FINDING THE SUPERMODEL IN YOU

FINDING THE SUPERMODEL IN YOU

THE INSIDER'S GUIDE TO TEEN MODELING

CLAUDIA MASON

FOREWORD BY
CAROLE WHITE

Skyhorse Publishing

Skyhorse Publishing books may be purchased in bulk at special discounts for sales promotion, corporate gifts, fund-raising, or educational purposes. Special editions can also be created to specifications. For details, contact the Special Sales Department, Skyhorse Publishing, 307 West 36th Street, 11th Floor, New York, NY 10018 or info@skyhorsepublishing.com.

Skyhorse® and Skyhorse Publishing® are registered trademarks of Skyhorse Publishing, Inc.®, a Delaware corporation.

Visit our website at www.skyhorsepublishing.com.

10 9 8 7 6 5 4 3 2 1

Library of Congress Cataloging-in-Publication Data is available on file.

Cover design by Brian Peterson
Cover photo credit Renée Cox

Print ISBN: 978-1-63450-494-2
Ebook ISBN: 978-1-5107-0163-2

Printed in China

It is with deep love that I dedicate this book to my mother, Diane Mason

TABLE OF CONTENTS

Acknowledgments • ix •

Foreword • xi •

Testimonials • xiii •

Introduction • xvii •

Chapter 1. In the Beginning • 1 •

Chapter 2. Launched into Outer Space • 19 •

Chapter 3. Take Grandma With You – a.k.a – The Chaperone • 41 •

Chapter 4. Navigating the Industry • 47 •

Chapter 5. The Wolves • 77 •

Chapter 6. Managing All That Money • 85 •

Chapter 7. Health, Fitness, and Natural Beauty Care Vs. Anorexia, Bulimia, and Meds • 103 •

Chapter 8. Sex, Drugs, and Rock 'n' Roll • 121 •

Chapter 9. College and Life After Modeling. Be Prepared. • 137 •

Chapter 10. Branding • 151 •

In Closing • 167 •

Claudia's Scoreboard • 169 •

Appendixes • 179 •

Photography Credits • 185 •

About the Author • 188 •

ACKNOWLEDGMENTS

It is with immense gratitude that I thank the following people who have contributed in their own way to this passion project of mine:

Alan Morell – my uber agent, guide, and brilliant idea man, who always has my back

Chris Owen – for his indefatigable support and spot-on judgment, there for me whenever I need him

The team at Skyhorse Publishing

Diane Mason – no words can describe my gratitude to my mother for her love and tireless devotion

The writers of the foreword and testimonials – Carole White, and Anna Sui, Christophe Kutner, Enrique Badulescu, Isaac Mizrahi, Mary Greenwell, Pamela Hanson, Paul Cavaco, Sam Mcknight, Sciascia Gambaccini

All the incredible photographers whose work appears in my book – Andre Rau, Andrew MacPherson, Angelo Pennetta, Avedon, Bolling Powell, Brendan Burke, Bruce Weber, Christophe Kutner, David Bailey, Dewey Nicks, Enrique Badulescu, Gilles Bensimon,

Acknowledgments

Guzman, Hannah Khymych, Javier Vallhonrat, Jim Varriale, Karl Lagerfeld, Marc Hispard, Mario Testino, Martin Brading, Matthew Rolston, Max Vadukul, Olivia Owen, Pamela Hanson, Patrick Demarchelier, Peter Lindbergh, Regan Cameron, Renee Cox, Robert Erdmann, Sante D'Orazio, Satoshi Saikusa, Scavullo, Thierry Legoues, Tiziano Magni, Tyen, Walter Chin, Wayne Maser, Willy Vanderperre

The magazines whose covers are shown in the book – *Vogue Paris, Vogue UK, Vogue España, W* magazine, *Elle UK,* French *Elle,* German *Elle, UK Cosmopolitan, Madame Figaro, Harper's & Queen, Mademoiselle, Miss Vogue*

My friends, my family, colleagues, and various professionals – Raphael Santin, Corinne Nicolas, Harvey Tanton, Olivia Owen, Claudine Ingeneri, Virginia Lisnow, Lorenzo Uras, Rene Bosne, Katy Strouk, Florence Lobet, Doreen Small, Michael Williams, Julian Peploe, Eric Rayvid, Michael Hoeg, Gabriel Rocha, Patty Sicular, Judy Mamelok, Kevin Jennings, Jack Best, Oscar Reyes, Patrick Lazhar, Photo Mission, Katrin Wesolowski, Phillipa Steele, Colleen O'Neill, Meredith Truax, Kenny Suleimanagich, Julius Poole, Rocco Licalsi

You have all been amazing!

FOREWORD

I had the great pleasure of being Claudia's agent in London. She is a fantastic model. They don't make them like her anymore. Claudia's exotic looks and statuesque frame put her on the top of all the clients' must-have lists throughout the world. She was a favorite of international fashion magazines including *Vogue, Harper's, Elle,* and *Marie-Claire*, as well as of the top advertising clients and all the great designers for Fashion Weeks in London, NY, Paris, and Milan. She was a true professional and made my job as an agent easy. Claudia has had a long career in the business and possesses intelligence, confidence, understanding, and a natural warmth. I can't imagine any other top model better suited to guiding young models.

Carole White
Premier Model Management Ltd, London
www.premiermodelmanagement.com
Model Agent and Author of *Have I Said Too Much* (Penguin Random House)

TESTIMONIALS

"It is with great pleasure that I recommend Claudia Mason's book. Claudia is certainly one of the true stars from the Supermodel Era. No one will ever forget her *Mademoiselle Grunge* cover from February 1993! I loved her in my clothes, and on my runway. She has had a long career in the business, and possesses intelligence, confidence, warmth, and dignity . . . I can't imagine anyone better suited to guide young models."

—Anna Sui, Fashion Designer

"The first time I met Claudia was on a shoot in Thailand. I remember when I first looked at her to be amazed at how superb she was. Since then I worked with her many more times. Because to me, she performed just like an actress would, taking on the different roles I asked her to portray for the camera. She always got right into the idea of the shot, we also had great fun on all the jobs we did around the world.

She's a top model who is smart and funny too, and knows with her friendship how to bring an extraordinary support to the whole team."

—Christophe Kutner, Photographer

"I always laughed so much with Claudia whenever we worked together. She has a great spirit and was wonderful to photograph. Not to mention the complete professional that she is."

—Enrique Badulescu, Photographer

"It was always so much fun to work with Claudia. She was one of the great models of the supermodel era, and gave a special smart quality to the clothes on the runway and in photos. She has a wonderful personality which adds to her great face and body, important qualities for me in a model. She just looks smart. Versatility is of the utmost importance in that field and I think Claudia really embodies that while remaining pretty neutral. She showed the clothes, which a lot of models don't care about, they care more about showing themselves. She's the definition of a pro and has had an amazing exemplary career and I think she would be the perfect guide for younger models today."

—Isaac Mizrahi, Fashion Designer

"No one would know better than Claudia to give advice on the world of modeling . . . she was such a great model herself! Smart, clever, and witty with a great face, she was able to adapt to whatever mood and look was desired in front of the camera. She was funny and bright and a joy to be around. We had great times together."

—Mary Greenwell, Makeup Artist

"I have worked with Claudia many times over the years. We first met in Paris in the 90s. Her beauty and spirit have always been an inspiration to me. She's a great model and a wonderful woman, always has been."

—Pamela Hanson, Photographer

"What makes Claudia Mason a great model is her ability to make us believe she is whatever character she is portraying in a photo or on the runway. She can project elegance, innocence, power, sweetness, sexiness, anything the clothes she is wearing call for. As an editor it is easy to use her for any shoot or put her in any designer's fashion show. She knows the nuances of how to hold her body, change her expression, alter her walk, so whoever sees the photo of her or the show she is in, believes she is the woman who actually owns the clothes she is modeling. I think she is able to do this because of her generous, open nature. It must allow her to feel whatever that woman must feel when she is in those clothes. Whatever the reason, it has allowed us to look at that incredible face for all these years—and I for one am happy I had the privilege to work with her."

—Paul Cavaco, Creative Director, *Allure* Magazine

"Claudia has always been a pleasure to work with. She's a fantastic model, and she's always been keenly aware of how to work her hair to enhance the outfits she was modeling, whether on set or on the catwalk."

—Sam McKnight, Hairstylist

"I worked with Claudia Mason on several shoots with top photographers during the late 90s, she was always hard working and dedicated, a pleasure to have around, funny and easy-going. She understood teamwork from a very young age and her commitment to the job was always remarkable. Claudia is a beautiful and well-mannered woman, and her compassionate nature makes her very special to me."

—Sciascia Gambaccini, Fashion Director, *Vanity Fair* Italia

INTRODUCTION

IN MY BOOK, *Finding the Supermodel in You,* I will be your trustworthy guide as I escort you through life experiences targeting your self-confidence and self-esteem, and using fashion and the modeling industry as our example and mutual gauge.

I was on the frontlines of fashion, and I survived. In fact, I thrived and had a ball, from being discovered at age thirteen at Tower Records in New York City's Lincoln Center district, not far from where I grew up, to becoming an international supermodel. I've graced *Vogue* covers, I've appeared in top advertising campaigns shot in the most exotic locales around the world, and I've walked down the catwalks of all the fashion greats, from Valentino to Calvin Klein, from Chanel to John Galliano. I'm here to help you and your parents navigate your way through what can often feel like the wilderness of modern teenage life, e.g., how to stay grounded in every circumstance, and how to measure risk so you can have fun without falling off a cliff. Useful advice in fact for everyone.

Through some of the glamorous, hilarious, and difficult stories from my career, I will share with you what it is really like to be a model. I will also share the invaluable lessons I have learned in my career. These lessons provided me with enormous self-confidence and sky-high self-esteem and they will apply to all teens and even to adults.

My advice to all of you grows out of my counsel to teens who want to pursue a modeling career. It was as a teen having to learn fast how to survive and succeed in the business world of fashion that I began to build a high degree of confidence and self-esteem. For would-be models, I will discuss why one should avoid the mall-type agencies; how to conduct oneself with one's much older foreign-speaking agent in "the City of Light"; and what to say and how to say it to anyone and everyone in the fashion world.

We know adolescents need mentors. Adults need mentors too. In our complex world full of nonstop responsibilities, appointments, deadlines, social media, events, etc., people can use all the help they can get navigating their way through.

Using the fashion industry as our gauge means we are talking about teens as the ones most needing guidance. They are the primary support of this industry in its constant push to sustain its glam image and maintain its high-profit bottom line. These pubescent girls and boys are the indispensable instruments which the fashion industry employs to revamp, reboot, revitalize, and promote their products. And it is worth mentioning that it is the only industry where the girls make more money than the boys, because the fashion industry is predominantly geared to a female market. Women's fashion is a vastly bigger business than men's fashion.

If a person is an instrument, and if that person is aged twelve to seventeen, then we must take into account the fact that we are dealing with someone who is not yet developed in the ways of the world. This person hasn't yet had to leave their parents' home and go out into the world of business and money. They haven't fully started to explore their sexuality, nor have they had to fend for themselves with regard to food, shelter, and paying bills. They are just beginning to know themselves as independent beings apart from their parents. They are in the earliest stages of adulthood. They need guidance from those who have been there before, especially if their parents are clueless to the inner workings of the entertainment industries. (Note: As of November 20, 2013, child models who live or work in New York State are covered by the labor law and regulations that protect child performers; New York labor law defines a child performer as anyone under the age of eighteen who renders artistic or creative services.) These industries, including sports, film, music, theatre, as well as fashion, operate in a high-paced "get-it-while-you-can" and "do-it-when-you're-young" environment. If you miss that specific window of opportunity, then your train most likely will not be coming back to the station. Today, as an example, the average model's career lasts around four years.

Ultimately though, it's case-by-case, as it all depends on the individual, which is true of any endeavor. It's about making connections and having a personality that will make you shine above the rest, and will translate to brands that will support a lengthy career. This puts even more pressure on a young person to perform well, and win the jobs and good graces of those adults around them who are the decision-makers in this arena that they have been thrust into.

Scary stuff for teens, as well as for their parents. What to do? Whom to trust? Where to go? To leave school or not? Where's the guarantee? Well, there is no guarantee in life for anything, but I would say your best bet in getting information about how to avoid the pitfalls is from someone who grew up in one of the most frenetic, international, multilingual, jet-setting industries. This is where I step in. I have been there.

And let me tell you, what I have learned in my years in this industry has given me enough confidence and self-esteem to bolster an army! As I've said before, the expertise I have to pass along to would-be models is equally relevant for all teens and also adults.

Modeling is an absolutely marvelous industry at best. I'd like to open its doors to you, take you on a tour, and provide you with the tools you'll need to take care of yourself no matter what circumstances you're in. Ultimately, I want you to have a wonderful time with whatever career you choose, and also learn to spend and save your money wisely.

Speaking of tools, one exciting feature of my book is the Scoreboard for success, a handy checklist for gauging your progress. While it is geared to models, it is an approach that can be useful to anyone.

All of this should be enjoyable! Get ready for a fantastic ride . . .

CHAPTER 1

IN THE BEGINNING

IT ALL STARTED IN A neighborhood that holds a lot of sentiment for me, Lincoln Center on Manhattan's Upper West Side. Walking down the street between 62nd and 66th Streets, and from Columbus Avenue to Broadway, is a nostalgic and a bit of a mystical experience for me. I feel as if I'm Philippe Petit, teetering on the tightrope between the joy and exuberance of my childhood love of dance, and my soul's endless yearning to express itself creatively in whatever artistic capacity it can find. As a child, I wanted to be one thing and one thing only: a prima ballerina. As I walk down those streets today, I feel transported to another time and space, as if dreaming, where I'm visiting an area from my youth that holds so much meaning and resonance for me, and is at once so familiar but so foreign to me now, remote from my present-day realities.

How can I begin to describe my passion for ballet? This beautiful, elegant, classical discipline so moved me as a child, that I felt intoxicated by its hold on me, often sobbing in the audience at a ballet performance, comforted only by the fact that I was in the dark, one of many viewers of the spectacle before me left alone to enjoy the sweet reverie. Any time I would watch a ballet performance, or see a dancer walk down the street, I felt stirred to perform. Whether viewing a performance by the New York City Ballet, or taking classes myself, it was the closest thing to God that I knew from a very early age. I was not raised in a religious household mind you, far from it. Although my mom is and was deeply spiritual, she had no interest in organized religion.

Neither did my dad, although he had been raised going to church as a boy. However the significance of a spiritual life was deeply rooted in me, even through the at-times tumultuous and emotionally difficult realities of my childhood household. My parents were intellectual bohemian artist types. My dad's a writer and had been a teacher, and my mom was a model and an actor as well as a writer. She was also an account executive for a media service for a number of years when she became a single mom needing to make ends meet. They were sophisticated New York City parents, both highly intelligent as well as highly intense people, both born and raised primarily in New York as well. They divorced when I was four years old and my mother raised me, with the help of my maternal grandparents. I saw my dad every other weekend. Fortunately, he lived only ten blocks away from us on the Upper West Side. I was born and raised in Manhattan, and if there is one place that can simultaneously energize and soothe me, it is New York City. Growing up in Manhattan was heaven for me. I loved every square inch of the city. There is so much going on at all times, and for a kid it is just one big playground. Concrete playground mostly, but playground nonetheless. Culturally it is a mecca and I was taken to the ballet, the opera, museums, art galleries, the Cloisters, you name it. I was exposed to so much, and I responded to all of it, but particularly to the performing arts. I've traveled around the world, and I've lived in other cities, but the Big Apple is truly where I feel the most alive. It is where I'm meant to be. And this vortex of creative, artistic energy around 66th Street and Broadway sweeps me up into its rapidly spinning core and doesn't let go of me. Oh, how delicious it is!

So there I was, all of thirteen years old, standing at 5'10" with a shoelace as a headband tied through my hair. This shoelace had little ice cream cone illustrations and was one of many shoelaces I used to decorate my hair back then. It was the hip, cool thing to do at the time, and I had laces with all kinds of illustrations, including puppies, Hello Kitty, and pointe shoes. I was with my school friend, Gidget, at Tower Records on 66th Street and Broadway: right there in the heart of the aforementioned intersection of my soul, where just across the street I had not too long before been a dance student at the prestigious School of American Ballet (SAB), George Balanchine's school that supplied the future stars of his New York City Ballet (NYCB) company. My quickly fading ballet career, which had once looked so promising, at least in my eyes, but was now a sputtering little flame trying to stay lit, was a sad reality for me. The fact was, I was too tall for NYCB's school, and I wasn't turned out enough at the hips, nor had I feet that were anywhere near what they needed to be for the demands of dancing on one's toes. So, one day after class,

My first modeling test, shot on the George Washington Bridge, NYC

3

miss
VOGUE

1/87
SEPTEMBER
DM 4,80
SFR 4.80
ÖS 38.–
HFL 5.80
LIT 4.800
PTS 400

JETZT WOLLEN WIR'S WISSEN!

LIEBE: Her mit den Gefühlen, Jungs!
+ Test: Wer ist der Richtige?

MODE: Mixen, wie es uns gefällt 100 Outfits – 1000 Looks

BERUF: So sind Träume machbar

CLIQUEN: Wir geben den Ton an

STARS: Billy+ andere Idole

NEU!

PREISE: ES GIBT VIEL ZU GEWINNEN

© Robert Erdmann

One of my early covers
for *Miss Vogue*

my teacher, the former ballet star Kay Mazzo, had a talk with me, or with my mother, I honestly can't remember since it was such devastating news for me at the time. Ms. Mazzo basically said, "Yet again, Claudia isn't ready to advance to B1 this semester (I had been left behind twice before in A2), and it would be hard for her to repeat A2 for a third time, as it would be demoralizing for her. She is welcome to if she so wishes, however, why doesn't she try modeling? She's so tall and beautiful, and ballet is a tough path. Her body isn't really built for it. But I think she'd make a fantastic model." No words could have been more horrible to hear. Not built for ballet, too tall for pointe. My worst nightmare come true: SAB was going to release me. After the three years of struggling in their ballet classes, through twisted ankles, and hairline fractures in my right foot, but nonetheless thrilled to be a student at the school—that was it. Over. Done. Slammed. I could hardly breathe. I remember the one good aspect of it all was the revelation that Ms. Mazzo thought I was beautiful! She was a woman who didn't smile very often. She was so serious and sometimes mean that I couldn't believe she had looked at me long enough to notice my beauty. "Why doesn't she model?" What?! I thought, when I want to dance?! What on Earth would I want to model for! This was tough news for a twelve-year-old, and I was crushed. I'll never forget my mom and I discussing this news in her bedroom. It was daytime, but it felt as though the skies were black outside her window. I was heartbroken, my dreams were crushed, even though I decided to carry on with my ballet classes somewhere else. The prestige of SAB with the possible entrée into NYCB was now behind me.

So, a year later, at age thirteen, I found myself flipping through records with my friend Gidget "the Midget," as we called her then because of her 4'11" stature. With braces on my teeth, a brace on my back due to my scoliosis—oh, I haven't told you about that yet!—and the shoelace in my hair, I turned to find a woman excitedly staring up at me who asked if I had ever considered modeling. She introduced herself and explained that she was a scout from the Elite modeling agency's petite division, and that she normally looks for shorter girls, but she saw me and had to approach me. She gave me her card and suggested that I have my parents call her and she would then send me on to the main offices of Elite. Now, you have to realize that I was standing next to "Gidget the Midget," who was petite, and Bonnie Winston, the scout from the petite division of Elite, not only didn't chat with Gidget, she didn't even give her the time of day. And to a thirteen-year-old, this is tough stuff. The only thing I was thinking about was would Gidget still be my friend in five minutes. We were in the same eighth grade class at the small private school, the Cathedral School of St. John the Divine, and Gidget was clearly insulted at Bonnie's dismissal of her. I played it cool with Bonnie, pocketed her card, said goodbye as she left us, and went back to browsing through tunes with

Gidget, swallowing back my excitement and pretending that it was no biggie as I sensed Gidget's jealousy immediately. Gidget was like, "You're not really gonna call are you?" And I was like, "I dunno, maybe I will, but whatev," feeling excited inside, but instinctively not wanting to show it. And sure enough, the next day at school, Gidget managed to turn the other eight girls in my class against me. Ah teenagers, you really are too much!

I had been teased and taunted as a child by the girls in my classes at all the schools I attended pre-high school. It was awful, and please know, if you're the target of bullying at school, remember it is because you look different and are beautiful, and they are jealous. You are also most likely tall and awkward, and so you stick out. Children can be very mean to one another, and the child or tween that is the most different from the pack will generally be the one to be picked on. Beautiful models often start out as awkward girls, with a certain beauty that hasn't yet fully bloomed, but is there. The ugly duckling story. We also might have braces on our teeth as well as on our backs. I certainly did. I not only had braces and a retainer as well as a night guard, but I have scoliosis and I also needed to wear a body brace from age twelve to eighteen. Being a teen can be murder. Being a supermodel on the rise made it easier in certain ways, but growing up in the fashion industry had its drawbacks as well, such as missing out on my adolescence. My scoliosis had been discovered by a fellow dance student at a summer ballet camp in Saratoga Springs, New York, when I was twelve years old. It turned out that I had an S-shaped curve in the thoracic and lumbar regions of my spine. Scoliosis is a lateral curvature of the spine that occurs when one side of the back muscles develop more than their counterpart muscles on the opposite side of the spine. It is most common in girls who grow fast (and boy did I, four inches in one year) although it affects boys as well, and it is usually hereditary.

Being in a body brace throughout my teen years was humbling. At first I had to wear the Boston Brace a total of twenty-two hours a day. I had only two hours out of it for showering and exercising. The time I could spend out of it was gradually increased until I stopped wearing it altogether when I was eighteen. This brace extended from my collar bone to below my tailbone. During my school years, when I wore the body brace, knock-knock jokes were directed at me by other students who would literally knock on it. But the jokes were funny and since I attended the small private Cathedral School, for grades six through eight, most of the kids were supportive of me and my brace-wearing self. I didn't get teased too much about it. Today, I find it highly amusing that I was not

John Casablancas parcourt avec Claudia Mason (la blonde) et Beverly Peele (la concurrente de Naomi Campbell) l'album de leur réussite.

Chloé
Régine

**92 BROMPTON ROAD, SW1
OPPOSITE HARRODS.
TEL: 01-589 2933.**

**35 BROOK STREET, W1
TEL: 01-409 1670.**

© Jim Varriale

only wearing a decorative shoelace in my hair and braces on my teeth when I was discovered by a modeling scout for the world's top modeling agency, but I also had a body brace on underneath my baggy clothes. Those scouts really know how to spot the pearl, don't they? I also walked into the Elite modeling agency wearing my body brace two months after I'd been scouted by them. This brace was a part of me at that time, and I never would have thought to remove it to go to a modeling agency. Modeling wasn't at all on my mind. I was a dancer and student and that was that. When I started to model, I was still under doctor's orders to wear my back brace for twenty-two hours a day. The fabulous Mario Testino, one of our industry's best photographers, would find it charming that I would arrive to his set at age fourteen, and announce to everyone that I had only a few hours out of my brace in which to shoot. The rest of the day, I would be in my brace throughout hair and makeup and lunch and downtime. In this respect, I was a rather unique phenomenon in the fast-paced fashion community. Fortunately for me, no one ever had a problem with my back brace requirements and my scoliosis had almost immediately improved to some degree from wearing it. This allowed for the hours spent out of the brace to become longer and longer, which freed up the shoot times on set. Not to mention my teenage dating life!

Some months after I had been scouted at Tower Records by Elite and just after I signed with them, a Ford Models scout approached me. Ford was Elite's only competition then, since the only two relevant agencies at that time were Elite and Ford. Sure there were a few other top-level agencies around, but in New York, there was Elite or there was Ford. No one else could touch them. They were both so exclusive and high end that it was like winning the lottery to be scouted by them. As I've said, I was oblivious to all of this at the time, but I do remember my mom being in a state of dumbfounded shock when I told her that I had been approached by an "E-light?" "E-lit?" scout. I was also clueless as to how to pronounce "elite." She looked at me with her jaw dropped, and said, "You mean Elite?!," and of course she pronounced it correctly. Bonnie Winston's card had sat on our living room bookshelf for a couple of months before we called and my dad finally took me in. My parents couldn't fathom how their gangly, braced-up, thirteen-year-old daughter could possibly be sought after by the Elite agency. My mother knew exactly who they were since she had done some modeling herself. My dad had always seen me as an actress, and was oblivious to the world of fashion and modeling. I was absolutely determined to follow up with Bonnie and see what would happen. I was curious about and captivated by the idea

One of my favorite photos from the beginning of my career. My ballet training leaps right through! A *Vogue* promotion.

of being a model because I loved to perform, and modeling is performing.
It is similar to dancing and acting, both of which I loved to do. I had already performed in school recitals and plays, as well as many shows for family where I cast my friends in the supporting roles to my starring role, and I wrote, choreographed, directed, and costume-designed the whole thing. I also performed many a night in front of my mirror. All of which later contributed to my ability to move effortlessly in front of the camera. It was a month before my fourteenth birthday when we finally went to Elite. Since my parents were protective of me, I was accompanied by my dad.

This is an important point for all of you parents reading this guide. You have to protect your teen from the get-go, as there are plenty of disreputable scouts out there who ask the talent for money up front. Reputable scouts never ask the talent directly for money for any service. Instead, they are paid by the modeling agencies they work with. There are also disreputable agencies. The mall-type agencies, for instance, are to be avoided. Don't waste your time or money bothering with modeling agencies that advertise in your local mall or online. Typically, they aren't legitimate. See the end of this book for a list of many of the top New York agencies. They have affiliate agencies in cities like Chicago, Los Angeles, or Miami for example. There are also good small-town modeling agencies that are connected to big city agencies, but research them before you enter into any type of negotiations or sign anything, which you legally can't do until you're eighteen anyway. With regard to signing contracts, you should always consult with a lawyer. If you're under eighteen, certainly if you're under sixteen, have a parent or guardian accompany you to an agency. Don't go by yourself, as I promise that you are not equipped to handle any negotiating on your own at that age.

On the topic of modeling schools, while the instruction they offer is not necessary for becoming a professional model, they can be helpful for girls who feel they could benefit from such training.

The only way you will have a legitimate modeling career is by walking yourself into a legitimate modeling agency or being discovered by one. You could be discovered as I had been, which is strictly up to fate. Traditionally, talent has been sought out by scouts. Recently however, at least one major modeling agency stopped scouting likely models the way they used to. Instead, they created an Instagram handle and hashtag which promises that if you tag your best selfie with this hashtag, you might be discovered by their scouts who regularly pick through the feed. You might also be discovered by participating in contests sponsored by legitimate agencies or professional talent associations. The steps to take if you choose to approach a legitimate agency are:

**K.L. by
Karl Lagerfeld**

Esilità alla Audrey
Hepburn. Bentor-
nato il piccolo abito ad
anfora con bustino senza
spalline. In cotone bleu
marine anche la cintura
alta. Scarpe di Joan and
David.

Rich Runaways

An exhilarating shoot for *Lei* magazine

- Research reputable agencies and make a list of them.

- Go to one of the agencies on your list with a parent or guardian during the open call times they give you on the phone or online.

- Don't spend money on professional photos before you go to the agency, since they will take pictures of you if they like you, and most likely will disregard and discard the ones you paid for and had done on your own. Simple photos of you taken on your smartphone for example are fine, at no cost to you, and easy enough to show to an agent if asked to. Remember, even though today's fashion publications are full of very retouched images of models, the more natural a girl can look in her photos, the better; no makeup or very little, and your own natural, clean hair. They want to see *you* in the photo as your beautiful, youthful, natural self and not some overly made-up vixen. Leave that up to the professional stylists once you're actually on set. One step at a time. The industry *loves* a fresh-faced teen, so you be you. And dress in your own clothes that make you feel most comfortable, a T-shirt and jeans are perfect.

- If they don't like you, don't get discouraged. Go to the next reputable agency on your list.

Don't give up hope if the top three agencies on your list don't want to sign you. There are others to check out. If there aren't many to choose from in your city or nearby city, then when you are able to leave your town, travel with a parent or guardian to one of the big cities, i.e., New York, Chicago, Miami, Los Angeles, Atlanta, or Paris, London, Milan, Sydney, Tokyo, and go to an open call. Contests are held throughout the world, and most likely in a city near you. The ones that you want to appear in are organized by the top international modeling agencies. Aspiring models are given a platform to be "discovered," with the ultimate prize being a signed contract with a leading agency. These contests are open to both recently discovered girls that the agency has in its new faces division, as well as to girls who are as yet undiscovered. Contests like the Elite Model Look have launched the careers of such supermodels as Cindy Crawford, Stephanie Seymour, Tatjana Patitz, and Gisele Bundchen.

It was a rainy day when my dad and I went to Elite. We'd gotten lost at one point and walked a few blocks in the rain. I remember walking along Park Avenue looking for the address, and noticing a big beautiful church and having a premonition that something extraordinary was about to happen to me. To this day, I can remember the sight of that church and the feeling that I had. I can still see the gray skies and the rain coming down on the sidewalk as we made our way east. Little did I know how much my life was about

Posing in a London studio for *Elle*   to change forever that day. It gives me chills to think about it. When we finally arrived and walked into their office, Bonnie Winston jumped up and grabbed me and introduced me to the rest of the agents present. I felt like a visiting royal, who receives the red carpet treatment and has adoring fans fawning over her wherever she goes. It was really quite something. I didn't know what to make of their excitement over me, but it sure felt great. They immediately called the main offices of Elite, which were in a different location, and set up an appointment for me to go there right away. It was thrilling for me, as I seemed to ignite the agents in both offices. This is what happens when a girl has just been discovered whose look is "the look" of the moment and of the time. It's really heady stuff. Walking into Elite's main office that afternoon was like a dream. It was so stylish and otherworldly to me, as I had never been in such an environment up until that point. It was on East 58th Street between Lexington and 3rd Avenue, I'll never forget, right next to Bloomingdale's. When you stepped off the elevator, you saw slick black walls and ceilings with chic well-placed lighting which highlighted the name "Elite Model Management." It was like a disco to me and I very much felt as if I had entered into adulthood as I stepped off the elevator and into this trance-like environment that immediately seduced me. Turning the corner and going through the glass doors into the lobby of the agency, one was greeted by all the framed covers of the supermodels of the day whom Elite represented, which hung on the wall behind the receptionist's desk. Wow. I suddenly wanted to be one of them and felt that I could be. I was intoxicated by the coolness, the grown-up feel, the sexiness and the romance of it, and I felt so excited by all the possibilities that might be in store for me. It was thrilling.

Modeling is a fantastic opportunity for a young girl to expand her horizons and see the world, especially if she is from a small town and hasn't been exposed to anything foreign, whether language or people or culture. It's also a fabulous way to earn a lot of money in a short amount of time. If you really want to be a model, then brace yourself for the ride, as it will be a rocket ship journey into another dimension from the world you've known up until then.

As you read my book, *Finding the Supermodel in You*, I will give you the positives and the negatives of what it's like to be a model, so you can avoid the pitfalls.

Following two pages: (Left) Italian *Vogue*—I love black and white

(Right) Sportmax—one of my first campaigns

In questa pagina: completo maschile revisionato: abbondante, senza spigoli né piega. Di lana grigia anche il pullover a coste. Pagina accanto: redingote alla caviglia: panno grigio con colletto a scialle in lapin blu notte. Blusa in lamé oro a collo alto. Guanti alla moschettiera in pelle e lapin.

TMAX

CHAPTER 2

LAUNCHED INTO OUTER SPACE

RECENTLY, WHILE BROWSING THROUGH MY Facebook page, I cracked up when I saw a comment from an old friend and former model, the gorgeous Scott Benoit. He was responding to my post of an interview that I had given to an online fashion blog which included some classic pictures from my early supermodel days. His comment was, "Don't forget about the ropes, Claudia." It made me smile, as it brought me right back to the great memories of the shoot to which he was referring that he and I were part of. The Versace advertising campaign with legendary photographer Richard Avedon, where I, along with Scott and the other four models that were also booked on the job, had to hang in different positions from thick long ropes that were suspended from the ceiling high above, all the while trying to look sexy, gorgeous, and cool, as if we weren't frightened for our lives. I thought I could join a circus after the acrobatics of that shoot! What a week it was.

But making the decision about whether or not I should take the job hadn't been that easy for me or for my parents. We were suddenly faced with making a choice that would disrupt my normal teenage existence. Remember, no matter how much you may want to be a model, this is not the sort of problem that the average teenager

ELLE

APRIL 1992

£1.60

SEX SURVEY RESULTS
WHY GIRLS ARE ON TOP

MAN OR MOUSE?
DISSECTING THE POST-FEMINIST MALE

JASPER CONRAN'S
BIG DRAMA

THE ULTIMATE GREEK ISLANDS GUIDE
PLUS...
WIN A HOLIDAY

ELEGANT
DRESSED UP TO THE NINETIES

© Andrew Macpherson

British *Elle* cover—totally elegant faces. As a society, we do not know how to prepare kids entering the entertainment industries about how to deal with the emotional difficulties they will face.

I was fourteen years old, barely acclimated to high school or to the modeling business that I had been suddenly thrust into, and I was shooting one of the most prestigious fashion campaigns on the planet—the Gianni Versace campaign. The photographer was the late great Richard Avedon, who was such an icon that when I was randomly asked back then which modeling job I was going to do next, people would just gape at me with their jaws dropped when I casually told them, "Oh, I'm shooting the Versace campaign with Avedon." I'll never forget the highly emotional conversations with my mother at the time right before the shoot, as to whether or not to take the job (I know I know, you're thinking was there even a question?!), since it was a shoot that would require me to miss one week of school. This was a slippery slope for me in those days, since I truly loved being with my friends in school and hanging out afterwards in places like Central Park's Sheep Meadow or the Bagel Nosh restaurant which was on Broadway and 69th Street at that time. The idea of missing out on a week's worth of schoolwork was also upsetting since it would set me behind, and I was not a straight-A student. I did well with the discipline and structure of a school week, I found it calming. Such was the effect my ballet class schedule had on me as well, and one that I was not wanting to give up for anything.

I was attending the famed Fiorello H. LaGuardia High School of Music & Art and Performing Arts as a dance major in my freshman year, and I wanted to stay in a daily school schedule as much as possible, since I so enjoyed being a teenager and spending time with my peers. I was at a crossroads over this decision to leave school for a week and do the shoot, and I remember sobbing over it to my mom in a restaurant on the Upper West Side, the neighborhood that I was raised in. "Oh mom, I'm so confused, what do I do . . . ?!" sob, sob, sob. I can get emotional at times! "Well," my mom started to say, with her usual look of anxiety, " . . . What do *you* want to do . . . ?" Ugh, not what I needed her to say . . . "I don't know!!!! That's what you're for—help me Mom . . . !!!"

This was so difficult for my mother, being put in a place of having to make decisions as to what would be the best choice for my present happiness and personal growth, as well as for my future. Now, who can ever make the "right" decisions on these big life questions, especially for another person that one is so intricately connected to as with one's own child? But I needed her help because I wasn't clearly pulled in one direction or the other. Even though I had always wanted to be a dancer, an actress, a performer, and as a model I loved getting made up to look like a glamour queen and wearing all those

ELLE

N° 2571

Cheveux

24
idées
pour
changer
de
tête

Préférez-vous
manger ou faire l'amour ?

Avec Caroline au Bal de la Rose à Monte-Carlo

M 1648 - 2571 - 13,00 F

HEBDOMADAIRE. 10 AVRIL 1995
90 FB. 6 FL. £ 2.25. 4,20 FS. 8 DM. AT S 55. CN $ 4.25. 4 200 L. 500 PTS. PORTUGAL CONT. 500 ESC. 800 DR. 27 DH. 2800 MIL. DOM 20 F. GABON 2500 F CFA. RCI 2400 F CFA. TOM 750 F CFP. USA $ 4.

Me in a wig—dramatic look!
French *Elle* cover

amazing clothes, I had never considered modeling as a profession and still didn't. It was never part of my consciousness. I think the first time I picked up an issue of *Vogue* was right after I had been discovered by the Elite scout. My mom had been a model, mostly for an illustrator, but she didn't bring fashion into the house. That wasn't our mojo. Ours was a home of art, intellect, spirituality, and macrobiotic eating that I raged against. So for me, as glamorous as this world that was pulling me to it was, my soul was still in the throes of a love affair with dance and the New York City Ballet. That was like oxygen for me. *That* I understood. Except, of course, I wasn't physically pliable enough nor had I been born with the right height nor kind of feet for the outrageous positions one's body has to be able to perform. I was still so wrapped up in it, and the world of fashion had not yet taken me over.

After deliberating back and forth for days, weeks possibly, about whether I should miss school for one week and take this opportunity of a lifetime, I finally decided—with my mom still unsure, although she had always said it was ultimately my decision, which was parentally wise of her (take note, moms out there)—that I would take it and everything would work out okay. I was going to enjoy it, and I knew I would once the job began, since I was going to be doing what I greatly enjoyed doing: performing! Albeit modeling, but at the top level for an iconic photographer, dressed in the best clothes and made up by the best hair and makeup team. I was spoiled from the start of my modeling career because I started off working with the *crème de la crème* of the fashion industry. I started at the top, and I loved all the hullaballoo around the sets and the production of shoots. I remember being handed a menu and being asked what I wanted for lunch by an on-set caterer, or studio assistant, on my very first modeling job at fourteen years old. I felt as if I had arrived into a whole other world than the one that I was used to. I grew up well, middle-class, went to good schools, and I was never in want of anything, but this was suddenly a different world from the one I was accustomed to, and it felt magical. It was something that I greatly looked forward to soon enough, as it was enchanting in a lot of ways, and it completely captured my imagination. But I remind you that I was one of the lucky ones in that I was handed the silver spoon by the fashion industry from the get-go. Not everyone is that lucky when embarking on a modeling career as a teen. That said, it was still difficult to navigate the hills and valleys of the industry emotionally, mentally, and physically.

Since I was in such high demand by the fashion industry, school was suddenly "interfering." I'll never forget at age fourteen or fifteen, when my parents and I were wooed at a dinner

Following page: What a gorgeous headdress for the cover of French *Elle*

ELLE

N° 2453

QUOI DE NEUF EN 93 ?

LES TENDANCES NOS CHOIX ET NOS AUDACES

SPÉCIAL ASTRO

VOS PRÉVISIONS SIGNE PAR SIGNE

36 PAGES A GARDER

M 1648 - 2453 - 13,00 F

HEBDOMADAIRE 4 JANVIER 1993
90 FB - 6 FL - 3,95 - 4,20 FS - 3,40 DM - AT 3 55 - CN $ 3,95 - 4 800 L - 475 PTS - 480 ESC - 500 DR - 22 DH - 2 300 - DOM 19,50 F - GABON 1500 F CFA - RCI 1000 F CFA - TOM 700 F CFA

© Gilles Bensimon

ELLE

by three of the top brass at Elite NY, the agency which had discovered and signed me. I was sought after by the upper echelons of the industry: designers like Karl Lagerfeld and Marc Jacobs, photographers like Mario Testino, Patrick Demarchelier, and Steven Meisel, magazines like *Vogue* and *Elle*, as well as clients like The Gap, Sportmax, and Revlon. They all wanted to work with me. Being in high demand meant I was a huge commodity to my agency which saw me as a big earner. School hours were getting in the way of work hours, so the agency invited my parents and me out to dinner to discuss the possibility of my leaving school and getting my GED. We were wined and dined and it was a very glamorous evening which I'll never forget. As we were on our way to meet them, my parents reminded me what the nature of the conversation would be. The agents were not just taking us out for a social hour. My mom and dad wanted me to realize that I would have to make a choice, and fast, as to whether or not I wanted to stay in school at my current high school or leave school and get my GED. This is not an easy decision for a kid or her parents to make. I felt the pressure, and I was torn.

My parents were a grounding force for me in a key way during those early years in the business. I wasn't the kid that felt comfortable leaving school and my whole life as I knew it, in exchange for modeling full time at fourteen. It felt intrinsically wrong. There is nothing wrong with it if you feel comfortable with the complete 180-degree turn your life takes, but you must be clear about the choice you make one way or the other. Having a solid family life grounds you. You have someone to turn to and rely on and get advice and support from even if they don't have all the answers. If you don't have a familial tie for support, then please seek out those you can trust to lean on who will give you valuable suggestions, as well as be there for you as an emotional support during the highs and lows that will come with the early years of teen modeling. The first couple of years are an out-of-your-skin experience that can be so intoxicating and stimulating that you will need to process all of it with a trusted friend, mentor, parent, or sibling. You are quite literally launched into another dimension, since life as you know it—school, boyfriends, parents' rules—quickly goes through an upheaval as you are now thrust into working in the glamorous fashion industry where you are seen as one of the glamorous people, and so your identity changes overnight. This can be tricky to deal with, as you may not know which side of the fence feels more comfortable. It's a dilemma for most kids in this position, whether they admit it or not. There is no right way to feel. The right way is the way that feels right for you, whether that is staying in school (but transferring to a school that lets you work during the school year, which is what I did), or dropping the school routine and getting your GED, as many of my modeling peers did.

Remember, even if you're longing to be a model, it still turns your life around. From more mundane situations like the agency wanting you to cut your hair from long to short (or to have bangs when you don't want to), to more challenging situations like whether or not you feel comfortable posing nude or topless, which is common in the industry. I'm speaking of course about artfully, tastefully done photos where usually only your breasts are shown, but still, this is not easy for all young teens. You must trust your gut and do what is best for you. You never have to pose in the nude if you don't want to. No one will force you to. As you get older, you'll most likely enjoy it. I did! Women's and men's bodies are beautiful, and most of us want to flaunt ours in front of the camera for the sensuality of the experience as well as for our posterity. All in all, there are different situations that could arise that are potentially emotionally traumatic for a teen to deal with.

I was one of the biggest Duran Duran fans out there when I was twelve. Theirs was the first concert that I went to at Madison Square Garden, and I was obsessed from that point on. My walls and ceilings were covered in posters of the group. Two years later, I was sent by my agency on a casting to meet Simon, John, and Nick to be the main girl in their upcoming video. I didn't know how to contain myself, and messed up the casting I'm sure, 'cause they were expecting a glamorous model to walk in, but I was still a kid who happened to be crazy about them and didn't know what to say. My point is that your world can be immediately turned upside down, and how you handle it depends on how grounded you are.

I transferred from LaGuardia High School of Music & Art and Performing Arts to the Professional Children's School, which allowed working kids time off from the regular school hours to work in their chosen fields, and to complete their missed classroom hours with correspondence work. (The "working kids" included Olympic athletes, ballerinas, classical musicians, opera singers, as well as actors and models.) But I still wanted to stay in a daily school schedule as much as possible, since I so enjoyed the life of being a teenager and spending time with my peers. I can't stress enough how important it is to follow your gut about whether or not to stay in a regular high school curriculum. Your career won't be lost if you feel you must have some regular high school experiences. Once you graduate at eighteen, you can hit the industry full time like I did, and fully enjoy yourself and your career. You will also be able to manage it better financially (see Chapter 6) as well as emotionally after the high school years are behind you.

Being flown to Paris, Milan, and London for modeling jobs as a young teen was exhilarating. I fell in love with each of these cities during my various experiences traipsing through them on the off hours away from the set, as well as through the wide range of wonderful characters I'd meet and work with, and situations I'd experience on set. The sight of Paris was pure magic for me, from the bridges over the River Seine, to the grand boulevards, and the exquisite design of the buildings, and indescribable charm of the narrow streets. The Paris Metro is delightful compared to the New York City subway, and I strongly encourage you to buy some "billets" (metro tickets), and make sure your mobile data, including GPS, on your smartphone works abroad, and enjoy hopping around the "City of Light" on the most efficient subway system that I've come across. When back on street level, stop at a corner brasserie or *tabac*, and have an espresso before continuing on your way. Until you have found your own favorite places in Paris, let me give you a few suggestions: For a total gym experience including a spa, check out L'Usine or Le Klay; for the trendiest department stores, the classics, Le Printemps and Le Bon Marche, are still the best; two popular restaurants I like are Monsieur Bleu and La Belle Epoque, although I also love the classic laid-back Brasserie Lipp as well as Café Flore across the street. Davé, the famous Chinese restaurant that is a Parisian institution particularly among the fashion set, remains one of my all time favorite places to dine in Paris. The French way of life is utterly delightful. London was heaven partly because I could speak my own language again, which was a relief after being in Paris or Milan. I speak French fluently, however there's nothing like speaking in your native tongue when you're away from home. London is so vibrant and full of gardens and exquisite museums and landmarks (the same can be said about Paris). Not to mention the pubs! If you need some time for yourself away from the job, go sit in Hyde Park, or see a performance at The Royal Albert Hall, or walk down the King's Road, and definitely check out Claridge's back bar. They have one of the best vodka cocktails I've ever had. In Milan, the great experiences are the people and the food! The Italians have a joy and ease about them that is a delight to be around, and their cuisine has always been my favorite. Be sure to check out the Duomo di Milano (Milan Cathedral) when there because it's a stunning sight to behold. It's such fun to be out of one's own environment where everything is exotic and seems so much more attractive—especially the guys! You won't usually have much downtime on location shoots, but if you do, be a tourist!

J'adore! **Such an honor to be a *Vogue Paris* cover girl.**

VOGUE
PARIS

OCT. F 40

Mode
Le blanc
couleur d'hiver
L'esprit
Carnaby Street

Bagages
De la malle
au petit sac
le cuir
en voyage

Exposition
Le journal peint
de Charlotte Salomon

T 5590 - 730 - 40,00 F

© Tyen

Versace These are international cities that have so much to offer, and the first few times you're in these fashion capitals will most likely be when you soak up the most. So go and explore.

A tale that will demonstrate some of the emotional difficulties that you could face as a model is set in Paris. I was eighteen years old and living there. I was in high demand at the time, and the head of the agency was monitoring my career like a hawk. Which was good, he was a modeling agent wizard just like his New York counterpart. Both men were brilliant at their jobs, and I was bringing in a lot of money for them, so I was a top priority.

He decided that my ears were a problem. Yes, my ears. They stuck out from my head at the top of the ear. I got these ears from my dad. They suited him, but on me they looked odd. Today it wouldn't be a problem. The current beauty standard isn't about "perfect-looking" glamazons as was the case when I was at the height of my career. Although a beautiful girl with no imperfections will never be out of style, fashion's compass changes with the wind, and what's considered "hot" today could be tomorrow's "passé," with very few exceptions. So the agency head told me my ears needed to be "pinned" back. I didn't like this idea at all. First I was told I had to lose weight, because even though I was always a skinny kid, I had puffed up a bit in high school from eating junk food. And now this.

I decided to go along with his suggestion and pin my ears back. Unfortunately, I didn't take his advice about which doctor to use, and insisted on going home to find a plastic surgeon in New York. It felt safer to do it at home, where I felt more secure about seeing a doctor, and where I'd also be accompanied by a family member or friend. Mistake. I ended up with the wrong doctor, and it is a shame what he did to my right ear in particular. He broke the cartilage, which dramatically changed the ear's appearance. Pinning back the ears is the simplest of all cosmetic surgeries, and yet I managed unwittingly to go to the worst doctor for this operation. I should have gotten the hint when I was told right off the bat by the woman at Elite who recommended him, that he was a great boob doctor. Take heed people, that was a hint to stay away. If you're going to get your ears pinned back, don't go to a doctor best known for breast augmentation. When it occurred to my parents to sue the doctor, it was too late. If anything like this should happen to you, and I hope it does not, be sure to initiate a suit before the statute of limitations runs out. I ended up going back to Paris with my tail between my legs, and the agent just shook his head and sent me straight to the French doctor that he had originally wanted me to go to, the one I should have gone to in the first place. He was the kindest doctor I've ever met. He thought what the American

GIANNI VERSACE

" The main themes
are hemlines and new shapes,
like a modern geometric kimono
and new versions of scalloped
hems. To me, long skirts
cannot possibly belong
to our times "

Brief wraparound
dress in grapefruit crepe,
with off-the-shoulder
overstitched collar,
held by a belt
with rhinestone belt loops,
by Ugo Correani,
Atelier Versace. Wool
crepe by Vivatex. Yellow
silk mules with multi-
coloured rhinestone
crosses. All by
Gianni Versace.
Scent: Gianni Versace

Legs in a little yellow dress. *Vogue.*

doctor had done to my ears was an outrage. Fortunately, it was just the right ear that had been badly affected. He did an excellent job of correcting it with flesh from my bikini line, which left barely a hint of a scar. Thank God I didn't get my nose or breasts done or anything else that is more prominent on one's face or body. Can you imagine the rage I would have felt if that had been botched? I spent one night in a Parisian hospital because I underwent a complex procedure involving both my ear and my bikini line. I made the mistake however of doing it alone in Paris and it was too traumatic a situation to handle by myself. I should have had one of my agents checking in on me. But I often tend to be too independent for my own good and not ask for help when I need it. It's important to voice your needs and concerns to your agents, especially when you're in a foreign city, and you need help. Whatever the need is, large or small, open your mouth and speak! You will feel much better once you do, and you will get many of your needs met which is very important for keeping a good, balanced, stress-free outlook and composure.

When I was sixteen, I did a shoot in Yemen, a country on the Arabian Peninsula. Talk about outer space! I thought New York summers were hot, but until I experienced a summer in the Arabian desert, I didn't know what heat was. On top of that, we were shooting fall/winter clothes. Several times I thought I'd pass out, and I was constantly thirsty for water. Avoid drinking water from the tap, especially in exotic countries. Sounds simple enough and obvious, but when you're running around the desert in the noon-day sun in a foreign land, shooting from dawn till dusk, jetlagged, and most likely underfed and dehydrated, you tend to act without thinking. *Well don't*, regarding drinking water. I learned this lesson in a country where I should have known better.

We had been shooting all day in the heat of the desert, such a different climate and landscape than that of the West. I was wiped out. Modeling is work! Make no mistake. It was summer, and I had been up since the crack of dawn posing in heavy clothes. In order for fall/winter clothes to arrive on the pages of fall/winter issues of magazines, you must shoot three to six months prior to publication. Yes, a drag, since that means posing in winter clothes for a shoot in the middle of summer, or vice versa. I've no preference for either since I feel any extreme weather deep in my bones. Back to my story: at some point I had a bad headache and rushed into the lobby bathroom of the 5-star hotel where we were shooting, and popped an aspirin into my mouth; then turned on the tap water in the fancy bathroom, cupped some of that water into my hand and swallowed the tablet. This one little action is what caused me to get hepatitis. I couldn't believe when the doctor at the American hospital in Paris later told me I had contracted it. I had started to look yellow, and my French agents were like, "Uh, somezing is wrung wiz your skeen darleeng, strahnge . . . And your eyes are yellow, thees is not goud . . ." You better believe it wasn't good! I felt awful while I was on the mend in Gay Paree. Fortunately, it was the lesser form of hepatitis, and it left my system soon enough. Again, you gotta take care of yourself, and be your own guardian on shoots in strange locales because there isn't anyone watching your back. It's good in a way because it forces you to grow up fast. You are suddenly thrust into the ever-moving business world, and you learn to swim in it—and fast. As long as you keep level-headed about it all, you'll sail more smoothly through the inevitable ups and downs.

Another experience comes to mind:

There I was, stranded on a deserted highway in Kauai, Hawaii, at midnight. I was alone, scared, and not sure how I had gotten myself into this situation. What had happened? I had just been flown over to Hawaii from New York on my own. I was fifteen years old, and how I had managed to convince my mother to let me go on the trip alone without a chaperone is beyond me. I must have really begged and pleaded not to have one, and I had good reason. This was an advertising campaign for Jimmy Z's surf clothes with the photographer Phillip Dixon. A fun campaign. I was to be modeling with a famous surfer who would be wearing the menswear line in the ads. I knew it was going to be a sexy kind of trip, in the sense that I was modeling sexy clothes in a sexy environment and I wasn't booked as the cute teenager. I was booked as the woman. This is where it gets challenging, girls and moms. We are teenagers when we start modeling at thirteen or fourteen. But what they are hiring you for at that age is women's clothing and you are expected to be sexy and alluring in front of the camera 'cause sex sells. Period. All of this is fine when you hit seventeen or eighteen, but when you're younger, it's difficult. At least it was for me, so don't think something is wrong with you if it's difficult for you too.

I knew that I could in no way have my mother there with me. I was still a virgin at this time, and it wasn't as though I was planning to let the hunky surfer dude deflower me in Kauai, but if there was any chance for a little action, I certainly didn't want her there. So, against her wishes, I went solo. I was an avid reader and my book of choice for the plane, besides the homework that I had to take with me, was Hemingway's *A Farewell to Arms*. I really enjoyed reading this novel. I loved the romantic story at the heart of the book. I felt that it was foretelling of all the possible romantic liaisons that I might be having in Hawaii. I was so boy crazy when I was a teen, just like any other teen, and I had such fantasies of love and lust running through my head all the time. But the truth is, as much as I wanted to have sex at that time, I wasn't emotionally ready for it.

I love this photo for Spanish *Vogue*—one of my all time favorite covers

If I'd see a guy I was attracted to, I'd melt inside but I wasn't able to compose myself around said guy, I'd be too nervous. I just wasn't ready. (For one thing, I was wearing a body brace for scoliosis most of the day.) There is no problem with this, and if you experience similar feelings, don't think there's something wrong with you. You never have to rush into having sex for the first time, or any time after for that matter. Have sex because you want to, and you are ready, and you feel comfortable enough to be intimate with the person you're choosing to have sex with.

I had my first significant boyfriend when I was fourteen years old and a freshman in high school, and I hadn't yet felt comfortable going all the way or even having oral sex for that matter. There is a time in life for everything, and you must trust your instinct and never feel compelled to do anything you don't innately feel comfortable doing. And never feel pressured into having sex in order to secure more work. That will only backfire in the end in ways that you couldn't foresee at the time. Although I still wasn't ready to have sex at fifteen, I certainly loved to fantasize about it! And I was so relieved that my mom refrained from forcing one of her chaperones on me this time. Chaperone energy would have ruined my ability to hold my own as an adult working with other adults. Although I was fifteen, I knew the kind of energy that there would be on the set, and I would have felt inhibited by a chaperone's presence, which would have affected my ability to perform. Yes, these are difficult decisions for parents and their teen children to make. There is no easy answer. You must do the best that you can for yourself in each particular situation and for each specific job.

My mother had always been anxious when I traveled alone. So imagine how she must have felt when she heard my voice from a pay phone (pre-cell phones, people!), telling her that I was stranded on an empty highway in Kauai and it was past midnight . . . Oh My God. My flight had safely landed in Kauai from JFK a few hours before, and

I had gotten my bag from baggage claim. I waited at the airport as I had been told to do by my agent for someone from the crew to pick me up and take me to the hotel. No one arrived, and when I called the number of the villa where we were booked to stay, I wasn't able to reach anyone. I started to get concerned, but didn't panic. I had the address, so I got myself into a taxi and figured that all was fine. At some point during the trip from the airport to the villa, the taxi driver seemed to have gotten lost. I kept noticing that we were on an empty highway for what seemed like an eternity, and I began to get nervous. I started to have doubts about the driver's trustworthiness, and finally asked him to stop and let me out near a pay phone, which he did. I still can't believe he left me there alone, I must have really ticked him off. I called the crew and they were upset to hear my news, and immediately sent someone out to find me. Then I called my mother. Oh boy. She was none too happy to hear the situation I was in. I could tell she was keeping as calm as she could on the phone, but I knew she must have been very upset, scared for my safety, and furious at herself for letting me travel alone.

How to avoid these pitfalls, moms? Well, the best way is to make sure that when your teen is traveling to a location shoot on her own, that not only is she equipped with all the necessary itinerary including contact information for the production crew, but that you obtain a copy too. That way if a situation should arise similar to the one I described above, you will be prepared and able to make calls and send texts or emails yourself.

The most fantastic helicopter ride I've had to date was on this shoot in Kauai. What a splendid sight it was as we approached a private beach that featured a magnificent waterfall. I'll never forget it. We were going to shoot one of the pictures for the campaign on that beach. It was where they had filmed the '70s version of King Kong with Jessica Lange and Jeff Bridges, and our hunky male model surfer dude was a raw, masculine type like Jeff had been in the film. I was gorgeously glammed out a la Jessica, and felt like a sex goddess in my outfit for the next shot. I was sitting next to the hunky surfer dude in the helicopter and he couldn't keep his eyes off me. Fashion shoots are always highly sensual. They are intoxicating and addictive environments, especially on the big money shoots where you're being treated like a queen all day and getting whatever you want, whenever you want it, brought to you by a production assistant. You look your best because you have the best hair and makeup team that has made you up, and you are wearing sexy clothing on your toned body—hot! And you can't help but feel it. Couple this with a sexy male model and a seductive location, and the set is sizzling! That helicopter ride was magnificent, and when we landed on the private beach, it was as if we had landed in paradise and we were the only human beings left on the planet. What a sight, what a ride, what an exhilarating shoot!

There have been so many out-of-this-world experiences that I've been privileged to have, thanks to my extraordinary career as a model. I've posed atop an elephant for a big campaign shoot in a photo studio in New York; I've danced on stage with the late Godfather of Soul, James Brown, in a Thierry Mugler fashion show in Paris; crossed the Nile River in a boat posing for the great Mario Testino, where once we got back to land, a local man desperately tried to convince Mario to accept thousands of camels in exchange for me; I was Giorgio Armani's dinner guest at his home in Pantelleria, the magnificent island off Sicily which happens to be two hours by boat from Africa, where I had lunch the next day. Etc.

And then there was the time I was arrested by the Parisian cops for being a hooker. Ha-ha! Well, I was almost arrested. Here's what happened. It had felt as though I had been waiting out on the street for eons. Where was he already? My date was late, and I was not too happy about it. I had waited upstairs in my apartment for well over half an hour for him to arrive before I got impatient and decided to wait downstairs on the street. It was a good neighborhood in Paris, the 1st arrondissement. I was pacing back and forth in front of my building in my high heels, short shorts, and a barely there top. It was nighttime, around 9 or 10 p.m. And I was in Paris living and working as a model. I had graduated from high school only months before.

I began noticing this one car that would appear and reappear down my quiet little street. Since I didn't know what my date's car looked like, I had been looking at all approaching cars with anticipation, hoping that my date had finally arrived. This one car started to slow down as it approached me, and the male driver looked at me as it passed me by. There was another man in the passenger seat. I didn't think much of it at first, however, after the third or fourth time they drove down my street, I got concerned. The street was empty, and I was in a foreign land after all. About the fifth time their car came down the street toward me, ever so slowly, I knew something was up. I ignored them. I had learned that from growing up in New York City, but when their car stopped right in front of me, I began to sweat. Both of them got out abruptly, walked up to me, quickly showed me their badges (they were undercover cops—great!), and started speaking to me rapidly in French. I knew how to speak French because I had taken it in high school with an excellent French teacher who had demanded that our

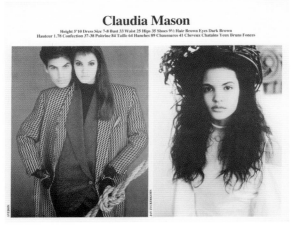

Claudia Mason

Height 5'10 Dress Size 7-8 Bust 33 Waist 25 Hips 35 Shoes 9½ Hair Brown Eyes Dark Brown
Hauteur 1.78 Confection 37-38 Poitrine 84 Taille 64 Hanches 89 Chaussures 41 Cheveux Chatains Yeux Bruns Foncés

My elite model card

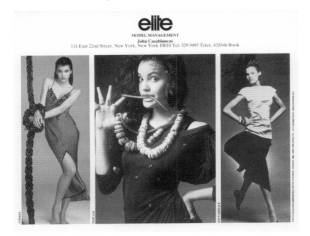

elite
MODEL MANAGEMENT
John Casablancas
111 East 22nd Street, New York, New York 10010 Tel: 529 9495 Telex: 428546 Book

Flip side of card

small class only speak French in her presence, no English allowed. Even though they were speaking so fast and in such an abrupt manner that I got flustered, I managed to communicate in French that I was an American model living in Paris in the building that I was standing in front of, and that I was simply waiting for my date to pick me up. They didn't buy it and asked to see my passport. I understood got from what they were saying to each other that they thought I was a prostitute, and they were going to arrest me. Wow. I must have looked pretty tarty. I guess it was that I had been waiting on that street for a long time, and that I looked with great expectancy at every car approaching. Funny to remember now, but I'm happy that I wasn't arrested. I had to go upstairs, with them following me, and show them my passport. It was so strange to suddenly have the police in my little studio-sized model's apartment. I was so pissed at my date.

If he had just been on time, none of this would have happened. When the cops finally realized I had told them the truth, they left. My date showed up shortly after that.

It's a tremendous advantage to know French or Italian. Should you ever be in a situation like this you can handle it more effectively.

CHAPTER 3

TAKE GRANDMA WITH YOU—AKA—THE CHAPERONE

SO, GRANDMA. OH MY GOD, there she was sitting like a stone statue on a little chair to the side in the studio. She was so uncomfortable, I was so uncomfortable. The whole thing was so uncomfortable and awkward and kind of unbearable. My Grandma Sophie was the light of my life when I was a little girl. She and Grandpa Leo could do no wrong, and I was the apple of their eye. I am so grateful that I had this great familial love in my life during my formative years. It helped shape who I was, and whom I would later become. I cannot overestimate the power of a grandparent's love, it is so rich and runs so deep. That said, the one person you do not want with you on a fashion shoot, watching over you like a hawk, staring down anyone who looks as though they might be mistreating you, not cracking a smile once, not even appearing to be breathing, is your Grams.

Wow, was I uncomfortable with her in the room! I felt as though I were in my bedroom making out with my high school boyfriend, and Grams was watching from the sidelines, as if she would blow the whistle at any moment she saw his hands go anywhere near me. Hysterical now to think about, but it was painful at the time. I was around fourteen, and the shoot was in San Francisco for a catalog. In the industry you either have editorial, advertising, or catalog, as far as photo shoots go. Editorial shoots showcase clothes of the current season in magazines in artful, highly creative photo layouts. Advertising refers to shoots for individual clients promoting their current collections for selling purposes—these campaigns can also be highly creative. Catalog shoots are typically more directly commercial rather than artful. In this instance, the catalog I was shooting for was Macy's West, and I had been flown out to San Fran for the shoot. Since I was a high school freshman, I wasn't allowed to travel alone. My mom wouldn't hear anything of my pleas to let me go by myself. I tried to convince her that I was sure that none of the "nice people" in the fashion industry whom we had met thus far would harm me. My mom just wasn't having it, and who can blame her? I was fourteen! I needed to have a chaperone, I can see this now, but at the time I was furious at her for insisting.

My mom couldn't always be my chaperone in those days because she was a working single mother. In fact most of the time during that period when she insisted on me being chaperoned to all of my out-of-town shoots, which was from age fourteen to seventeen, she was not able to go herself. One time a relative had been sent along as my chaperone. It had been challenging for me since our personalities were so different. Unfortunately, there were some clashes between us and a general feeling on my part of wanting to run as far away from her as I could. Then there had been the friend of a friend of my mom's, another difficult coupling for me, since this woman was odd, and seemingly jealous of me, which created such an awful edge considering we had to live in the same small apartment together in Paris for the fourteen-day shoot schedule that I had been flown over there for. I think she had been solely interested in being flown to Paris on my mother's dime and seemed annoyed with having to spend any of her time there with me.

Some of these episodes are a little blurry in my mind now because they were so extremely uncomfortable at the time. My mom and I fought and fought over this whole chaperone issue. I felt like I was being spied on, and that I wasn't being trusted in my self-care abilities, which were sufficiently advanced, or so I had thought at age fifteen. I'm a good girl, I'd think to myself, which my mom knew. Why couldn't she just chill and trust that I knew how to take care of myself? I was a Manhattan-born-and-raised kid after all. What's not to know? A NYC kid gets to be street-smart fast, that's just how it is. Growing up in such a crazy, crowded, and diverse city gives you survival tools that can be used anywhere on the planet, no joke. Especially if you grew up taking the subway as I did. Well, what self-respecting city kid doesn't, right?

I'll never forget how I learned to take the subway alone. I've often told this story when asked how I could possibly have grown up in Manhattan. I was fourteen and I had been modeling up a storm from the get-go. Part of a model's life is castings and go-sees. A casting is when a client is calling a model in for a specific job. A go-see is when the agency arranges for clients to meet a specific model for projects in general. I had to go around on these castings and go-sees in the beginning just like any model does, and present myself to the clients as they looked through my modeling portfolio. By "present," I mean stand there and try and have a casual conversation with the prospective client, who most likely will ask you any number of questions from how tall you are to what your favorite band is, to how old you are and where you're from. Clients also love to know a model's ethnic background, as it is a look-based industry, and if they can't tell just by looking at you, then they will ask you straight out. Don't be thrown, they're not trying to give you the third degree even though it can seem like that at times. You must remember that in this context you are an object, and you are being scrutinized by these professionals who are trying to determine whether your look will sell their brand and bring in lots of revenue for their company. That's all it comes down to at the end of the day: $$$. If you don't get the job, it's not because of you personally, you're just not what they're looking for. So, in order to get around for my appointments, I had to be able to take the subway on my own. Up until that point I had always gone with adults or a group of friends, but not by myself.

It was the summer before high school, and my dad was the one for the job since my mom would have messed up the lesson out of sheer nervousness. Moms out there, please don't be overbearing worriers to your daughters when they're getting started in the industry. They need to feel that you know they are capable of taking sufficient care of themselves, which I'm sure most of you have prepared them to be able to do. You can't smother them with your own fears, as this is a surefire way to instill self-doubt and also cause them to disassociate from you, and who wants any of that? Back to the subway lesson. My father and I entered the subway without much discussion about how he was going to teach me to ride it alone. Which was very smart on his part, as I was then relaxed about the whole thing. He and I stood on the platform, and he told me what our final stop would be and that we would need to transfer at Times Square and that he'd always be only one train car away, and that we'd reunite on the street at our final destination. At that point he took up a position about five yards away from me. This is how we waited for the train, and I knew that he would be in the next car from me throughout the trip. When I exited the train at our predetermined transfer stop of Times Square, I saw him exiting as well. He looked to make sure I was there and pointed in the direction of where we were headed, nodded, and we continued in this way until we reconvened as planned at our final destination on the street. I felt completely chilled about riding the subways alone after this one lesson with my dad.

When you're under eighteen, a chaperone is warranted because you're still essentially a child who is suddenly thrust into an adult milieu in a very fast-paced business. The chaperone gives you the protection you need when you're learning the ropes, until you become confident enough to negotiate the fashion industry on your own. Another reason to have a chaperone accompany you on shoots away from home is that it can get lonely on the road by yourself when you're a teen. Especially when you're booked on a job where you're the only model. You need someone to keep you company, to talk to, to process your experiences with.

Speaking of processing one's experiences, I so enjoyed the moments with my mom post-job, when I'd come home and excitedly tell her all of the fun stuff that had happened during the day's shoot. I'd act out (with accents as well) all of the characters that I came across in the various professions of the industry, the makeup artists, the stylists, the photographers, and the designers. There were always terrific stories from the set that I couldn't share with my classmates, since the girls were jealous of me, and the boys didn't know how to talk to me, so I unleashed the stories onto my mom or dad. It was a great release, and it helped to process the day before I had to return to schoolwork and the norms of being a high school teen. It is very difficult to go from high fashion model back to schoolgirl and then back to model, at fifteen. Fact is there was nothing normal about my adolescence since I was a much sought-after model all over the globe. I cherished the grounding times that my mom and relatives provided. Girls can be swept away by this business, and I don't mean in a good way. Ideally, parents provide stability for the times when you're inappropriately approached by a photographer or agent or someone else who is not out for your best interests but has an agenda of their own. Again, this is part of the business world, but when you're under eighteen there is no way you would be able to finesse your way on your own through the adult situations that arise. And no one loves you like your parents, so try and be grateful for their support and care, as it is only in your own best interest. Of course there are also mothers out there who push their daughters to have sex with the men who can advance their careers, encouraging them to do drugs and party it up. I personally witnessed three such mothers when I was a teen model and, young as I was, I felt heartbroken for their clearly confused daughters, who were in much pain. I think the life of one of these young women was ruined.

If, for whatever reason, you don't have a mother who can act as your chaperone, then perhaps you have an aunt, sibling, or other relative who can. It's important for you to have an adult present to help you with the many decisions that must be made which arise from modeling as a teen.

It's not only on set where you'll need a guardian, it's in other areas as well. For instance, when you first approach an agency or are approached by an agency's scout, it's important to make sure it's a legitimate modeling agency and not a mall-type agency, since the latter doesn't meet the industry's professional standards, and how would you know this on your own if you're thirteen, fourteen? Adult guidance is of paramount importance in these situations. Trust me, as a young teen you are not at all equipped to handle on your own the many challenges that arise in this industry. There will be plenty of untrustworthy people out there who will try to take advantage of you physically and financially and in any other way you can think of. You can use all the protection you can get until you are capable of dealing with these challenges on your own.

If you're from a small town and you're desperate to get to the nearest big city to attend an open call at a legitimate modeling agency, go with an adult. If a relative or trusted older friend isn't available, then how about a teacher, guidance counselor, or other mentor? You'll have a much better chance of avoiding potential pitfalls and positioning yourself well with adult guidance rather than by trying to go it alone. The industry insiders will most likely treat you better if they see that you have mature people around that care about you and understand what's going on. Remember, neither your agents nor the clients are responsible for your emotional wellbeing. That's not how it works for any person in any profession. That is up to you, which is all the more reason why you need support, because you are too young to manage the psychological demands that will be placed upon you as a natural by-product of the business. You will most likely not understand this or agree with this as a young teen, but you will appreciate it later on when you're an adult and on your own, trust me.

Remember that to the extent you're able to treat the chaperone situation with grace and humor, you will be far ahead of the game.

Lastly, for those of you who don't have a good relationship with your parents and are unable to turn to them for love, guidance, and support, rest easy. Figure out who you can turn to as I'm sure there is someone in your family, community, or school who would be there for you, and seek comfort and support with them. There are also wonderful programs such as Alateen that provide caring, supportive communities where you can seek help.

CHAPTER 4
NAVIGATING THE INDUSTRY

I'VE GRACED THE COVERS OF *Vogue, Elle,* and *W* magazines among many others. I've shot major ad campaigns for Revlon, Versace, and Fendi among others. I've worked with the most distinguished names in the fashion world repeatedly. I've been kissed on the cheek by Bono backstage when hanging out with U2 after their concert in LA, had Duran Duran's Nick Rhodes and Simon Le Bon as dinner guests for my birthday party in Milan, had a very senior Gregory Peck stare at me from across the foyer at an exclusive party held at a chateau outside of Paris, and exclaim to me when he approached me that I was to be an actress. I had heard those same words from Charlotte Rampling at another party outside of Paris. As well as have a much older Terence Stamp write me the loveliest note asking me if I'd like to date him, after we had been seated next to one another at the British Fashion Awards dinner in London. I've also had Ron Wood of the Rolling Stones draw my portrait at a party in NYC. I've certainly been a very lucky girl.

But don't be fooled, modeling is also hard work. The glamorous part is just one aspect of being a highly sought-after model. The fashion industry is fast-paced and very competitive. To become successful, you have to present yourself to your best advantage and learn how to deal with the variety of business and creative types you will be

istante

BOUTIQUE: MILANO, VIA SAN PIETRO ALL'ORTO 11 - TEL. 02/76014544

Christy, Naomi, and me for the Istante campaign

meeting and the many challenging situations you may be confronted with.

How to navigate through it all?

For one thing, be yourself with everyone you come across in the industry, whether it's a famous photographer whom you've been dying to work with, or a movie star whom you've been seated next to at an exclusive event. This is show biz, essentially fun stuff, so enjoy it all, including the talent that you are. Get used to the attention, and be appreciative of it. Be assertive when needed without being offensive. It's the difference between behaving like an entitled child or a teen who will be developing into a responsible adult. Party and have a good time but also remember that this is part of your profession now. Make that profession last for as long as possible. Take the best possible care of yourself, which includes getting enough rest and remaining alert. Always show up to work on time. When you're out and about at industry events like awards shows, dinner parties, and other exclusive occasions, you're socializing and enjoying yourself sure, but you're also promoting yourself. Models need to be experienced in person as well as in images and fleeting runway appearances to make the strongest possible impression on the powers that be who hire them. Our business is a social business, don't forget. Public relations is a very important aspect of it, so you'll want to get your face out there as much as possible. Accept invitations to movie premiers, award shows, store openings, dinner parties, fundraisers, etc. Once you start making enough money, you might want to hire a publicist to keep your name circulating to the max.

The first time Giorgio Armani saw me, he exclaimed how beautiful I was. It was a moment I'll never forget. I was sent to see him for his upcoming *prêt-à-porter* fashion show in Milan, and I had to walk down the runway in his Via Borgonuovo showroom in a flesh-colored body suit and tights with full hair and makeup. This was so he could see how I looked and walked on a runway without the aid of clothes. There were other models there going through the same inspection, but I somehow felt confident that once he saw me he would immediately book me for his show, and that is what happened. Confidence in yourself is very important for succeeding in this industry, so you want to go about building your confidence in any way that works for you. Feeling good about how you look and how well you move is a major confidence builder, so take good care of your face and body. Practice positive thinking. Recall a moment in your life when you did something that made you feel proud, or when you were complimented for some achievement,

Following two pages: (Left) Five fresh faces, left to right: Eva Herzigova, Beverly Peele, Petra Lindblad, me, Nadja Auermann

(Right) My first *Vogue* cover. Beyond thrilling.

VOGUE

JAN
£2·50

**Fresh faces
new choices**

© Peter Lindbergh, British Vogue cover, January 1992

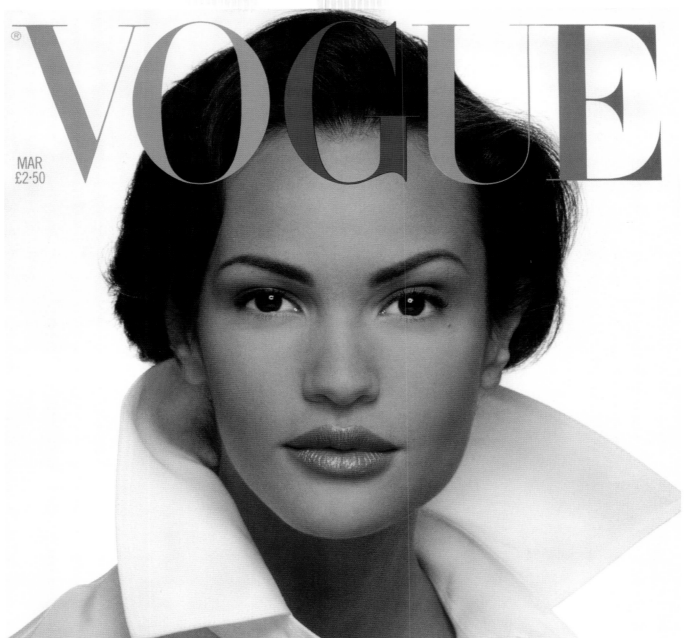

VOGUE

MAR
£2·50

The strongest looks from the
international
collections . . .
the blues, the whites, the stripes...
beauty 2000
where to expect breakthroughs

LOUIS VUITTON

Twin me. Expressing my punk side for Louis Vuitton.

however small, or when you were engaged in a pleasurable activity. The "will-to-good" is a useful spiritual concept to call upon when needing to summon the best of yourself and others in order to achieve your goals. Briefly, it's the energy that identifies with the greater good in every situation. Cultivating tools like these will also be helpful when you are faced with rejection, an inevitable part of any business and especially the entertainment industries. Anyway, I walked for many an Armani fashion show since that moment with Signor Armani, and I had the privilege of sitting next to him at a dinner party at one of his homes. He is the complete gentleman, and I thoroughly enjoyed the time I spent working and socializing with him.

The way to relate to the extraordinary designers that you will have the good fortune to work with is to remember that they are people too. Yes, they are extremely talented fashion designers who are known throughout the world, but they are also your business associates. Your distinctive roles serve the larger whole of the immense fashion industry. The same goes for the fashion stylists, the magazine editors, the hair and makeup teams, the art directors, and the photographers. Everyone has a specific role to play in achieving the industry's goals and yours is to wear the designs and make them look their best to capture the imaginations of as many potential consumers as possible. How you learn to model is mostly by working as a model, *voilà*. Like most careers in the entertainment industry, you essentially learn on the job, and the more work you do, the freer and more expressive you become in front of the camera. It's truly that simple, just like riding a bike. The more top-tier photographers and creative teams you work with, the more you learn to refine your image and technique, so to speak. As you gain experience expressing yourself for the camera, you will learn which parts of yourself to bring out to suit the job at hand. Modeling for an editorial spread is different than for a catalog shoot or an ad campaign, although sometimes these differences are very subtle. But the more work you do, the more confidence you will acquire, which will enable you to shine like the star that you are in front of the camera, and you'll discover parts of yourself that might never have emerged if it wasn't for modeling. How exciting!

There is so much you can learn from the successful sophisticates you'll be working directly with in this industry as well as from a wide range of other interesting people, from around the world, with whom you might otherwise never have crossed paths. Be alert to what they can all teach you, not only about being a model, but also about how to get along with all kinds of people, about the ins and outs of business, and about life in general. Take full advantage of all the information and experiences and insight you'll be privy to that can help you grow as a person and contribute to your consideration in time of educational and career options when you will no longer be modeling. This period of your life can afford you a serious education of its own kind if you remain curious and alert.

There are four annual "fashion week" seasons: two *prêt-à-porter* seasons and two haute couture seasons, one each of spring/summer and fall/winter. *Prêt-à-porter* takes place during a month-long period for one week each in NY, London, Milan, and Paris. Haute couture is held in Paris for one week. These seasons, particularly prêt, present a distinct challenge to a model. The work is practically 24/7. A model hardly has time to sleep between the fittings, shows, dinners, and parties that are part of the demands of her job. It's a full-on speeding train ride through four different cities, where you are dealing with four different agencies across four different cultures, and all of the designers and creative teams in between. It's enough to make your head spin off your body. You are subsisting mostly on adrenaline, but as exhausted as you might become, it can still be highly entertaining and provide you with a tremendous opportunity for personal growth. At least in retrospect!

They would "ooh la la" and "tut-tut-tut," with their mouths turned down at the corners. Their eyes would roll upward to the good Lord, and their hands holding little pins would suddenly jab you, or be thrown up in the air in a gesture of sheer exasperation, as if they were your irascible neighbor who has dragged you to court for the 50 millionth time over your not respecting how to properly dispose of your trash, however tidily you have disposed of it time and again . . . Let me introduce you to the French seamstress. *Voilà . . . !* She is all of 4'10," if that, typically round in shape, and as fiery and ill-tempered as Satan himself. Ooh la la indeed. These women drove me crazy when I was doing the top fashion shows around the world and would arrive in Paris for fashion week, looking forward to all the excitement, only to deflate the moment I stood in front of the martinet of seamstresses, *à la française!* They make it seem as though you are a CIA spy and hence a traitor if you so much as put on an ounce of weight, therefore changing your waist size by an infinitesimal degree, your hip size by the tiniest margin, your breast size from an A to a slightly swollen A, and your head size from something altogether different in size and shape from yesterday, however impossible that might be. It somehow happened, according to them, and it was all your fault you terrible creature. *"Mais, comment c'est possible . . ?! Mais c'est pas vrai Veronique ohhhh . . . ."* the seamstress

LOUIS VUITTON

fitting you would glance over to her peer and say, "*c'est vachement PAS possible* . . . ." as she'd glaringly look up at

you and then back to Veronique, and carry on insulting you to her colleague, assuming that you didn't speak French. (Translation: "But, how is this possible?! But this isn't true Veronique ohhhh . . . " "This is really NOT possible . . . ")

Ah, oui. You have to deal with these difficult women during fashion week, as well as many other often volatile personalities occupying the various positions in a designer's team that make it possible for a design house to survive in the cutthroat, seasonally changing world of fashion. It's important for you to understand however—as I finally did—that the seamstresses are fundamentally stressed-out and overworked. They want to finish their endless, thankless chores of sewing and adjusting and readjusting, and get home to their families at some point in the overlong workdays. Since you can't escape them anyway, take this as an opportunity to learn patience and compassion.

Fashion week is indeed a runaway train on speed, and it never stops long enough at a station for anyone to breathe, eat, bathe, or scream. It just keeps on going . . . All the way from NY to London to Milan to Paris. My friends, the four weeks or so of the international four-city tour of the twice annual *prêt-à-porter* fashion weeks are not for the faint of heart. You must be in your best shape, your top form, to survive just a few days never mind a few weeks of each fall/winter and spring/summer season. This is where a model is truly tested. Think of yourself as an athlete, an NBA player in Game 7 of the Finals. Everything is on the line, and it is up to you to perform at your best. That is what the fashion community that has opened its privileged gates to you is expecting, your A game out there on the runway, looking every bit the queen that you are, and that you must be, even when you don't feel it inside. You are a performer on a large stage when you walk the catwalk. All eyes are on you, from the front-row heavy hitters of fashion's elite, to pedestrians in Beijing watching live on a big screen. You are performing and selling the vision the designer and his team have created, which they hope will sufficiently impress the magazines, stores, websites, blogs, etc. To widely circulate and promote it to a broad base of consumers. Again, this is a business, in the end it's all about the $. So remember not to take any of the sometimes cruelty of fashion week to heart, it's not about you!

We would have to wait around at Saint Laurent *par exemple*, for hours on end. Waiting to be fit for his upcoming couture show. The twice annual *prêt-à-porter* shows plus the twice annual haute couture shows make it a nonstop fashion party practically all year round; although the couture shows are produced only in Paris,

En 1996, Louis Vuitton célèbre le 100ème anniversaire du Monogram LV.
Cette toile légendaire inspire des créateurs résolument situés à l'avant-garde de la mode : Azzedine Alaïa,
Manolo Blahnik, Romeo Gigli, Helmut Lang, Isaac Mizrahi, Sybilla, Vivienne Westwood.

CLUB MONACO

SILK SHIRT $59
FLIP SKIRT $49
BIKER JACKET $359

© Wayne Maser

as opposed to the *prêt* shows, at least the major ones, which are in Milan, London, Paris, and New York. The shows were always a time to look forward to as well as to dread, as it was an opportunity to reunite with all of your industry peers and buddies. The parties, the dinners, the men lavishing gifts, flowers, and promises upon us, ah, fun times. The designers would book us in advance, so we'd be met at the airport by a personal driver for that week and taken directly to a fitting at a designer's studio or a meeting with our local agent or directly to a show itself in some rare cases, where the fitting would occur as soon as we arrived, and then we'd be put into hair and makeup and sent off to the catwalk. That could happen only during the *prêt-a-porter* seasons, as the haute couture looks demanded much more time and effort of the seamstresses as well as of the whole design team. The documentary that portrays this very well is *The Last Emperor*, about one of the last great designers of the old guard, Valentino. I had the pleasure of working with him, as well as with the late great Yves Saint Laurent when he was still at the helm of his own line, even though advanced illness had greatly debilitated him.

I remember being pretty wiped out at a fitting for Saint Laurent's haute couture show one season. I had been eating mostly fruits, nuts, and Salad Nicoise (a fully balanced dish) for days before in anticipation of the shows. I had also exercised every day for around ten days prior, and here I was in my white robe, black sheer hose, and black heels, with the staple of the YSL look: a beautiful red-stained mouth, hair pulled way up and tightly back in a ponytail or chignon. It was at the famous YSL atelier on Avenue Marceau in the 16th arrondissement. I had been waiting my turn for my fitting, and there were quite a lot of other girls waiting too. At YSL it was an all-day affair, that's how they conducted their fittings, and if you didn't like it, too bad. If you were booked for the show, you had to sit around dressed in the aforementioned regalia, waiting, waiting, waiting your turn to be fit and presented to Monsieur Saint Laurent and his creative team. In fashion, you will often find yourself waiting around. Instead of reacting to the tedium, once again use this as an opportunity to grow your patience skills. And have your smartphone or Kindle or other reading material at hand, or crossword puzzles or whatever suits you.

I had been quietly reading as I sat in a chair in the hair and makeup room. We had to get full hair and makeup for Saint Laurent fittings as well as for those of Valentino and a few other designers. They wanted to see how their clothes looked on us with full hair

FERRE JEANS

Evening Silhouettes:
Redingote and Dressing-gown

©Pamela Hanson

Claudia Mason

Previous page: Mario Testino happened to be where we were shooting for German Vogue. Such a great moment captured on film.

and makeup, that's just the way they did it. We would also need to walk up and down an area set up like a mini-catwalk in some cases, so they could really get a feel for how a particular look would appear in the actual show. It was time consuming and a pain in the ass to me at the time, but there was also something old Hollywood about it and, since this is rarely done anymore, I'm glad I got to experience this special time in fashion history, where I had the privilege of working with the great master designers who had dressed some of the world's most glamorous divas of the stage, screen, and social worlds. I felt like I was now a part of this elite inner circle of fashion history, and it was a delightful perspective that brightened up the more mundane and superficial aspects of the job.

I often brought a piece of fruit and a bag of mixed nuts with raisins. I seemed to live on those items during fashion week work hours, after hours I let loose. I knew that I had to remain skinny 365 days a year, 'cause you never knew when you would be called to the set. Even on vacation, I'd generally watch what I ate, and if I had decided to pig out, which for me meant consuming bread, pasta, cakes, beer as opposed to wine, I'd calculate for how long I could do this before I'd have to cut that food out again, and get back down to hirable shape and size.

When I finally got past the Saint Laurent seamstresses poking me and pinching what little extra flesh I might have had, accompanied by their exasperated sighs and comments, and after my makeup was perfectly placed on my face, my hair sprayed to within an inch of its life with the ever-fashionable Elnett (the decades-long staple of every hairstylist), I was buttoned up in my now perfectly fit-to-me-in-that-moment-don't-breathe-or-a-button-might-pop-off-and-cause-a-fuss-in-the-changing-room garment. If a button did pop off, the seamstresses would be called in to remedy the situation at once, and they would give you the evil eye as they quickly rattled off in French how this clearly was your fault for instantaneously gaining weight, as they defended themselves and their work to the impatiently waiting creative team that sat or stood on either side of M. Saint Laurent. When all of this mayhem and drama was behind me, and I would actually be standing in front of M. Yves Saint Laurent, in designs of his that he had personally chosen for me to wear, it was exhilarating. It was a mini-performance, as I would walk a bit for him then stand and casually pose as was expected of me. He would always look up at me and say, "*Elle est belle, elle est magnifique.*" What a compliment from such a legendary dressmaker. He would approve my outfit, or decide on an adjustment to the hem or sleeve length or style, but he always smiled

Hanging with Gary Cherone of Extreme and Rossy de Palma for American Vogue

62

at me. I felt like the most beautiful girl in the world in those moments. It was also inspiring to have the great Loulou de la Falaise, who was part of his design team, there. She was a beautiful woman who possessed such an innate sense of style. She was inherently kind and had a certain grace and ease about her that was always a comfort to me. Whether standing or sitting next to M. Saint Laurent, she'd smoke her cigarette through an elegant holder, as she languidly looked you over and waited for the master's approval.

It's important to know that very often the creative teams that work with the designers are the same people who are hired to create the looks for advertising campaigns and editorial shoots and magazine covers. You want to always remember that the creative director for a fashion show might be recommending you the next day for that particular designer's advertising campaign. Creative directors, stylists, producers, and casting directors work a myriad of jobs in the fashion industry, so develop relationships with them on whatever job you happen to be since they most likely will be the reason you're hired for the next job, and on and on. In this way, the business is small. So avoid burning any bridges.

The man behind the man (Saint Laurent) was a certain Monsieur Pierre Bergé. M. Bergé had a personality style all his own. I distinctly remember how he would control the runway lineup of the Saint Laurent couture shows. M. Bergé was a short man who possessed the bearing of an army general at war. He would stand backstage right in front of the monitor that displayed the show live, just behind the stylish curtain that separated the backstage area from the audience, and fiercely grip the skinny upper arm of the model that was next to go out onstage. His eyes would be glued to the screen, not to the models whose arms he would be draining of blood, his grasp so firm that it could be really painful. You would do the best you could, as you didn't want to upset this man. You would stand there, barely breathing, staring ahead, taking quick dart-like glances at him, praying he wouldn't lock eyes with you, or, alternatively, hoping to meet his stare with a smile to warm his heart, however much you knew you were seriously fantasizing in that moment. You wanted him to let you go already, as he pushed you a little forward, then changed his mind and pulled you back, then pushed you a little forward again, while you tottered back and forth on your high heels that were either too big or too small for you. The shoe sizes are always off for the shows, don't ask me why. Be prepared! It drove all of us models crazy. Either you were stuffing your shoes (if they weren't open toe of course; if they were open toe—good luck!) with anything you could find: paper, plastic, cotton, or you were in excru-ciating pain because the shoes were too small. At the moment when M. Bergé decided to have you walk out

A divine shoot in Greece for *Harper's Bazaar*

Elegance with an easy feel. Opposite page: Black cotton/Lycra low-cut bathing suit with white embroidery, about $522, and matching fringed shawl by Norma Kamali. This page: Ivory cotton sleeveless tunic with stand-up collar, about $485, and matching slim trousers, about $375, from Anne Klein Collection by Louis Dell'Olio. Sandals, 9 West.

© Patrick Demarchelier

onto the catwalk, he'd push you forward almost to the edge of the curtain where you would be visible to the audience, THEN release his grip and command you to "*Allez!*" ("Go!") I would feel like I'd been released from rope bondage and was now about to walk the plank. Needless to say, he was not a happy-go-lucky kind of guy. I was nervous to step out onto a YSL haute couture runway, which for the fall/winter collection had required me to take off my gloves, scarf, and coat, hold them in one hand gracefully and manage not drop any of them while keeping my bag held lightly in my hand, all the while looking as cool as Audrey Hepburn in *Breakfast at Tiffany's*, as I glided down the runway and showed off the fine feathers I was decked out in. I was nonetheless relieved to be out of this man's iron grip.

Cool, cool, cool is the name of the game. Never let 'em see you sweat. A model on a runway, particularly a Parisian haute couture runway, is a woman of sophistication, grace, elegance, and cool, a fantasy portrayed to sell this image to the woman who could buy these clothes, and some of those buyers are right there in the front row. Designers at the great fashion houses like Saint Laurent might change, and styles come and go, but within the fashion industry, cool is never out of style. I don't care how many times the style of the runway walk changes, or the look of the models on the catwalk, one thing will always stay constant, and that is the cool. You gotta have it girls, it's the essence of fashion.

When I arrived in Paris for the first time I was floored that they sold beer and wine in their McDonald's. Alcohol at Mickey D's?! Crazy. Everything was so exotic and lovely. The Parisians are not the friendliest of people, and I believe it's because their city has been unrivaled in aesthetic grandeur for so long in terms of its architecture, gastronomy, art, and fashion that they can get away with being snobs. It's almost as though they feel they've earned it. I fell in love with Paris despite the natives. As I began to make my way around this marvel of a place, I found that I really took to the Parisian way of doing things. Such as having separate food markets for the different food groups: *une épicerie* for general items including household supplies, *une fromagerie* for your dairy, *une boulangerie* for your baked goods, *une charcuterie* for your meat, and so on. It just thrilled me, and made so much sense re: freshness and quality. Of course big supermarkets have been around for a long time in Paris, but I avoided them as much as I could when I first lived there because the little separate shops held such charm for me and shopping in them made me feel like a real native!

The only blight was the attitude of the Parisians. I loved the French language. I had taken it in high school with an excellent teacher and so had a basic grasp of it when I arrived in Paris to

Sitting pretty in Greece for Harper's Bazaar

stay after graduation, and was delighted to use it in getting about town. But nothing had prepared me for *l'attitude des Parisiens*. They are in a class by themselves, and let me be clear: I am not talking about the French in general, just the Parisians. When I used my decent-enough French at a shop counter, the clerk would turn her head away, nose in the air, and call out "*la prochaine!*" (next!) as I stood there waiting for an answer to my perfectly innocent question of, "Where's the makeup remover please?" It's as if they detested tall, striking-looking foreign girls who didn't have a perfect grasp of their language. They certainly knew we came to their city to work as models, and they seemed to resent the sight of us. I had thought I was prepared, since I'd been an A student in French class for three years prior. But what I couldn't have foreseen was the manner in which so many Parisians tended to deal with one another as well as with foreigners, especially foreigners they didn't approve of for whatever reasons. As soon as I discovered that my polite schoolgirl approach to asking for help throughout the city was getting me nowhere, I decided to mimic the style I observed many Parisians use with one another: a direct, brash approach, a la the cigar-smoking men behind the bars in the tabacs. I started asking questions of supermarket workers and pharmacy staff in a tone that sounded like a local plumber, and suddenly the whole population responded to me as though I had suddenly stepped into the light. Ah ha! I got you, you silly Parisians, I would think to myself, you are going to deal with me now! And from that point on I had a fabulous time getting around town. I had found my Parisian sea legs.

It was interesting for me to realize that even when speaking to an English-speaking Parisian who didn't expect me to speak to her in French and who was supposedly "there" for me, problems still could arise. Enter "Justine," my agent. Ooh la la indeed. She was something else. I had just moved to Paris, it was the fall after graduation, and I was used to being treated as an incoming royal wherever I went on the fashion globe. Clients as well as my international agents were always thrilled to see me and chat and comment on how lovely I looked and what an exciting career I was having, etc. However Justine was my booker at Elite Paris, the Parisian Offices of the Elite agency that had discovered me in NY. You see, I'd started off in this business with a bang at fourteen, but since my parents and I had decided that I should not leave school for modeling, I'd only been working part-time until I graduated at eighteen. Although I was still considered supermodel material, four years had passed and I was told I needed to spend some time in Paris to prove myself again to the international fashion community who had been so interested in me at the start. They would hopefully have the same interest in me now.

Working the Versace runway

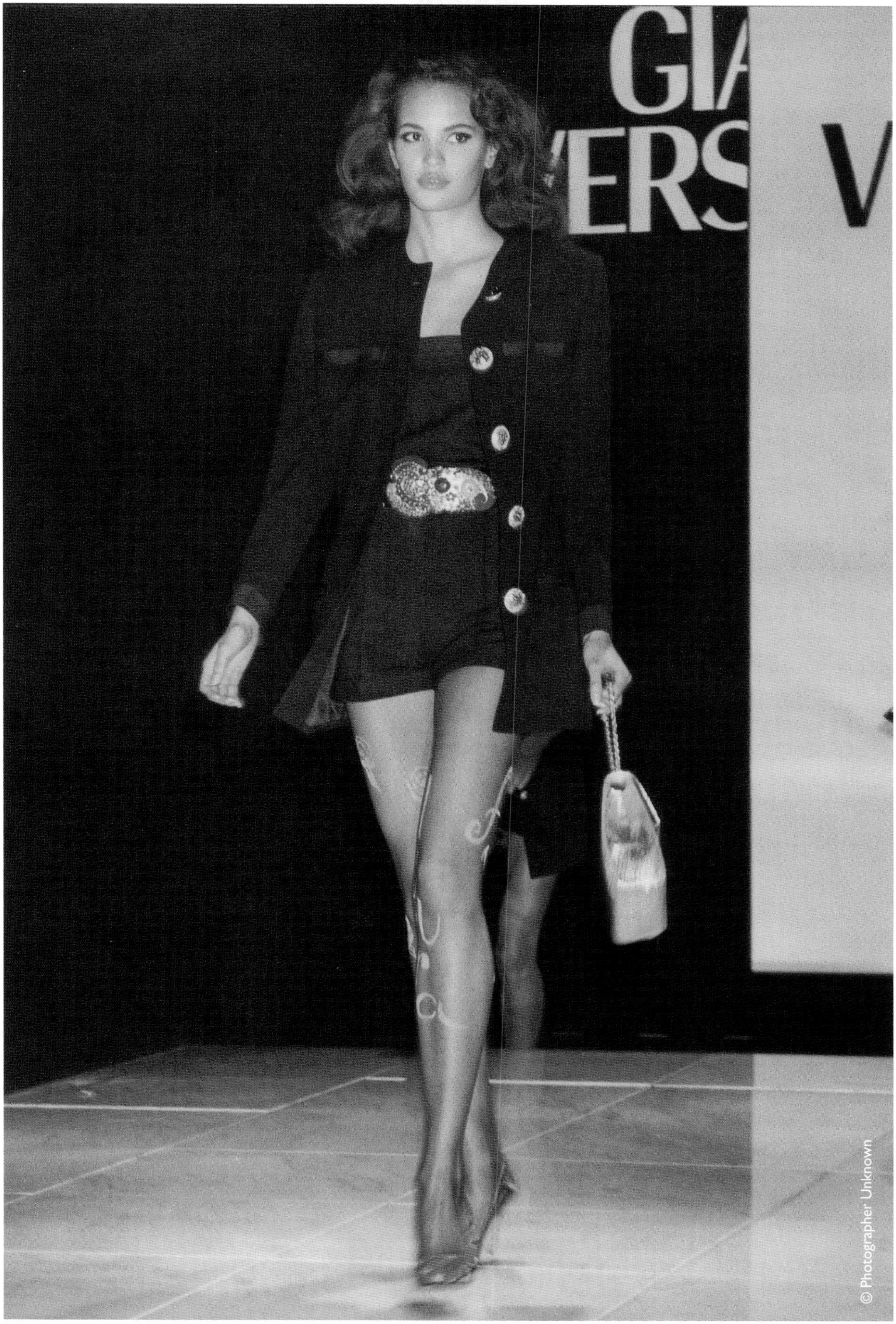
GIA
VERS
V

EVERY WHICH WAY AND LOOSE

Underlining this season's diversity, one girl (Shana Zadrick) and three hairstyles. For Chanel, *above*, hairdresser Julien d'Ys followed the sleek, straight and narrow. At Vivienne Westwood, *opposite, top centre*, Sam McKnight unearthed the crimping irons, and at Michael Kors, *opposite, top right*, New York's Oribe constructed a mass of feminine tendrils and tumbling curls. Take your pick.

WILD THINGS

Not since the musical *Hair* have explosively fleecy locks of this nature been seen on the international fashion scene. Unbound and untamed, curly, frizzy hair ran amok on the catwalks at Mizrahi, *above left and above*, Galliano, Chloé and Westwood. The age of Aquarius, it seems, is still dawning. If the Mizrahi examples seem unwearable – remember this was a show – look again at Chanel, *below*, where with the taming addition of a hat and less outlandish make-up, the result is charmingly feminine rather than strictly club-land.
Use: a diffuser on the end of your blow dryer and L'Oréal's Pumping Curls.

SOFT RED

Red lipstick, the catwalk classic, hasn't been eclipsed. It's still there as the most glamorously sophisticated and womanly option – see Claudia Mason, *above*, and Christy Turlington, *left*, both at Valentino. But in keeping with the trend towards lighter, brighter colours this summer's red is softer, more coral, glossier.
Use: YSL's Spicy Red Sheer Conditioning Lipstick; Guerlain's Paprike Rouge Sublime; Givenchy's Coralline 83 or 84.

107

Top models, left to right: Shana Zadrick, Meghan Douglas, Naomi Campbell, Christy Turlington, me, & Nadja Auermann showing top looks from the runway

The wonderful Monique Pillard, vice president of Elite New York at that time, who immediately saw my potential and had taken me under her wing when Elite had discovered me, told me on one of the many occasions she took me out to dinner with my dad that she believed I'd only have to stay in Paris for six months to get the ball moving again in the quick frenetic "they HAVE to have you and ONLY you for this job or they will DIE . . . " kind of way that I had experienced as a newbie in the business. And then I'd be able to move back to NY a bona fide star. In those days a model had to do time in Paris, she had to prove herself in Europe, and the capital of European fashion is Paris. Sometimes the hot city is London, but Paris and London are a short distance from one another, and once you're a model based in Paris, the other European fashion cities, London, Milan, Munich, etc., are not far away, and you can work the international European circuit quite easily. I found it a joy to hop on a flight to Germany from Charles de Gaulle Aéroport at 7 a.m., and be able to be on set in a Hamburg studio by 9 a.m., that particular flight being under an hour. I would make it back to Paris for dinner that night depending on how quickly the shoot day had gone.

Justine was one of those agents that are unfortunately out there, but fortunately for me I haven't run across too much. She was one of the many women who were sleeping with a particular European agency head. She was jealous of other females he was attracted to and his appetite was vast. Happily, I was on this fabulous career track and was not pressured to sleep with anyone in order to get more work kind of thing. My career was A list from the start. I've often wondered if the "casting bed" was something I could have stomached if I'd "had" to. I don't think so. Certainly not at that age. I'm grateful that I never had to find out.

I had a bumpy beginning to my Parisian life because I had to lose some weight and emotionally get into being a full-time model for the very first time. Justine didn't make it any easier, since she was not at all into guiding and supporting me. She never advised me about how to lose weight, or how to be strong and carry on with certain challenging clients. Instead she was negative about everything. As soon as I felt she was starting to get in the way of my career, I resolved to do something about it. I decided to speak to the director of the agency, after all he was the top guy there, and I had always been taken care of by the top agents in NY and knew my value in the business. I walked into his office and told him that I was not at all happy with how Justine was managing my career. I stated that I was an important model in the business

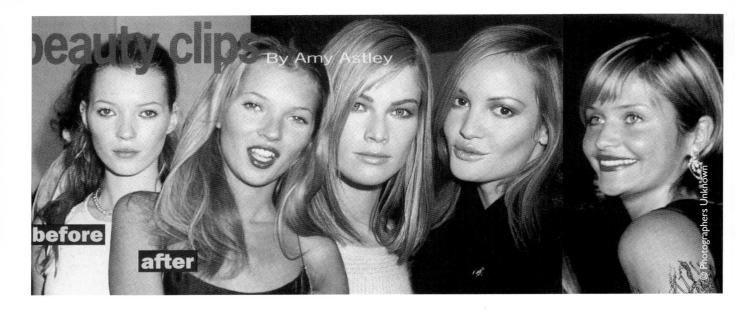

beauty clips

By Amy Astley

before

after

Supermodels with super highlights: Kate Moss, Meghan Douglas, me, Helena Christensen

with a track record, and that I was about to be the next hot thing again, so what was he going to do about it. Wow. When I write this I'm reminded of the courage I possessed at eighteen. You gotta have courage in this industry people, it's essential. He told me years later that he was impressed by me that day in his office, and knew that everything I told him was true and he was going to do his best for me, which is exactly what he did. What's important to remember is that you have to stand up for yourself. Not in an entitled way, but in an honest way, with all the facts behind you. Don't be timid with the fashion folk. Just as kids do in the playground, business people respond to bravery and strength.

You have to develop your relationships with the key booker on the board as well as with your own booker if they happen to be two different people at your modeling agency. The bookers, or model managers as they're also called today, are your main connection to jobs. Your agency represents you and pushes for you to get work. However, they also have the clients' interests in mind since they take commissions from both you and the client. Your booker will also most likely be representing a handful of other models, so you want to stand out in his/her mind as a model who is professional and easy to deal with and not an egomaniacal vampire. Go out for coffee or lunch with her when you can, and certainly be in touch with your booker on a daily basis. Get to know her without becoming a friend, per se. Friendship might naturally develop and very often does, which is fine, but remember, a booker is a business associate who is working for you and the agency that employs them. When they get you work, the agency makes money. You want to be gracious in your relationship with your booker.

For instance, if he or she has made you a lot of money in the previous year, it's advisable to get them a gift for Christmas. And remember you might not particularly like all of your bookers around the globe, but they represent you and part of being in any business is learning how to get along as best you can with everyone you work with, especially the people who are representing you to clients and who are on the phone pitching you for the jobs. You want to make your booker think of you first when they are suggesting models to clients for jobs. If you find yourself working with one who is not treating you with respect and you feel this can have a detrimental effect on your career, then by all means handle the situation. As tactfully as you can, but handle it. This might even include speaking to the director or head of the agency about being switched to another booker if you can't handle the situation on your own.

I'll never forget when I stepped into Industria Studio in NY for the Anne Klein A Line advertising campaign shoot with the world renowned photographer Steven Klein, and saw an elephant on set. OMG!? I thought to myself. Will I have to ride that beast?! My heart started beating faster and I started to sweat. I'm not that great with big animals that can crush me if they choose to. Little furry friends like dogs and cats are fine, but elephants and horses make me jittery. There was an elephant trainer present who was in charge of keeping the elephant subdued and focused but she was so much smaller than the animal that I had visions of her being run over as it headed for me. Clearly I was ill at ease about working with an elephant! I soon discovered there were two more trainers in the studio to help if need be, and I began to calm down. To my delight the elephant turned out to be gentle and easy to work with. Of course this was after she (yes the elephant was a she in my memory) had a mini-tantrum and all three trainers had to work pretty hard to keep her under control, and once she was, she took the biggest dump I ever saw in my life right in the middle of the set. Hilarious!

When it came time to pose with Mlle. Elephant, they brought out a ladder for me to climb to mount her. My heart started racing again and my palms got sweaty, but once atop her all was calm and we were a very compatible pair as we posed for the camera. There were some moments when she got frisky and made some big booming sounds (out of her trunk thank God) and I had to remain poised and sexy while Steven clicked away. Unfortunately the client chose not to run images of the elephant and me. A shame since I'd love to have seen them. The other shots from that campaign are some of my favorite ever. In one I was on a swing that was suspended high up in the air, also requiring a ladder to reach it. You must remember to breathe during any and all moments that make you nervous on set. You will most likely work with animals

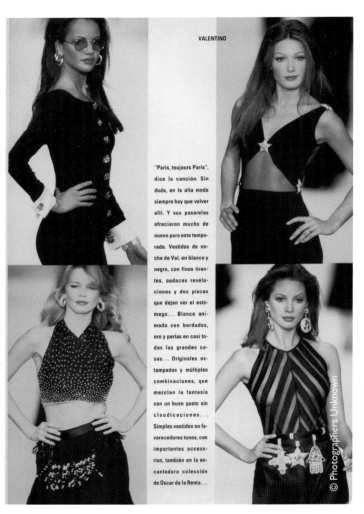

VALENTINO

"Paris, toujours Paris", dice la canción. Sin duda, en la alta moda siempre hay que volver allí. Y sus pasarelas ofrecieron mucho de nuevo para esta temporada. Vestidos de noche de Val, en blanco y negro, con finos tirantes, audaces revelaciones y dos piezas que dejan ver el estómago... Blanco animado con bordados, oro y perlas en casi todas las grandes casas... Originales estampados y múltiples combinaciones, que mezclan la fantasía con un buen gusto sin claudicaciones... Simples vestidos en favorecedores tonos, con importantes accesorios, también en la encantadora colección de Oscar de la Renta...

© Photographers Unknown

The Supers strutting on the catwalk, left to right: me, Carla Bruni, Claudia Schiffer, and Christy Turlington.

VOGUE'S VIEW

SAILOR CHIC

Ralph Lauren

Christian Lacroix

Ralph Lauren

rigueur for women in every port of call from Newport to Antibes.

According to Christian Lacroix, "Sailor style evokes the charm of resort life between the wars, when women began wearing men's clothes with a certain elegance." For spring Yves Saint Laurent swipes the yachtsman's blazer, transforming it into a crisply tailored double-breasted suit. Ralph Lauren takes a more direct tack, designing the actual uniforms for the America 3 racing syndicate and using them as inspiration for his spring collection. Despite the changing currents of fashion, there is even something left of good old John Cox Stevens in this newfangled nautical look—capped off as it is by the ubiquitous yachting cap.

VOGUE'S VIEW ▶ 236

Ralph Lauren   Ralph Lauren   Yves Saint Laurent   Christian Lacroix

Roxanne Lowit–Guy Marineau

So many great fashion show memories with my fellow catwalkers, left to right: Nadege du Bospertus, Christy Turlington, Karen Mulder, and me.

at some point and if you're uneasy around them you need to find a way to ground yourself and make friends with them as best you can. In these situations I automatically get very still and focus on my breath, beginning by breathing deeply. I mentally and vocally send loving words and thoughts to the animal and slowly approach to pet it so it knows I'm not there to harm it in any way. Most of the time they are more afraid of us than we are of them, so collect yourself by calming yourself down. And remember, a little shot of whiskey always helps if all else fails!

A short note about forming a models' union:

The idea of forming a union for models has been discussed for many years. It would function like the union that actors have long had. I don't believe that having a union to collectively address models' issues would give the model any more power over clients than actors have over producers. It would negotiate fair treatment for models in the workplace and provide medical insurance. I believe that a union for models would benefit the fashion industry since it could prevent some of the consequences of unmet needs from spilling over into models' work. It would give models a sense of meaningfulness as workers. Collective self-empowerment is a good thing.

CHAPTER 5

THE WOLVES

SO THERE I WAS IN the hair and makeup room of the biggest fashion studio in Milan, all of fifteen years old. I had just run into this empty room to take off my body brace, since we were about to start shooting, and the changing area where all the outfits were kept was also in this room. I was busy unfastening my brace, which I wore from age twelve to eighteen for my scoliosis, when suddenly someone grabbed me by the arms and pulled me to him. My head popped up and in no time I felt a big wet kiss on my mouth, as well as a tongue trying to wedge itself between my lips. Within seconds I felt his hard-on. OMG?! And oh no, it was the photographer! Oh my God! I thought, as I panicked and stood paralyzed like a deer in headlights. He finally released me from the grip he had on my arms, and I remained motionless, unable to look directly at him. He stared at me intently and then swiftly left the room, walking back into the main part of the studio which was just outside the changing room. Now what do I do? To make matters worse, my mother was just outside the room where he had pounced on me. Can you imagine if she had walked in on him mid-launch? I shuddered at the thought. You guys, I was fifteen years old, still a virgin, although I had a boyfriend back home. I had been flown to Milan, with my mother accompanying me as my chaperone, to shoot a highly prestigious editorial spread for one of the leading Italian fashion magazines. The photographer was one of the most important fashion photographers at that time, and it was all very glamorous. I now had to go and pose for his camera, while remaining as calm and relaxed as I could as he snapped away. This was not easy. I knew that I couldn't tell a soul at that moment, or for the rest of the shoot. I didn't even know if I should tell my mom, and if I did tell her, then when? And what would she do? I didn't want her to make a fuss and jeopardize my career, as I was already keenly aware that you have to handle these situations as coolly as possible, hysterics won't do. I also felt that if I told my agents, they would express momentary concern, but wouldn't have been able to do anything because this photographer was so powerful in the business, and my agency wouldn't have wanted to ruffle any feathers. This is a business after all, with a lot of money and prestige on the line. Fortunately, in recent years models have been more successful in having bona fide issues attended to. The Model Alliance (MA), which is a not-for-profit labor group for models working in the American fashion industry, seeks to improve the American modeling industry by empowering models themselves. Today, models feel more emboldened to speak out about inappropriate behavior or abuse of any kind they feel they have to put up with. So I carried on as best I could for the duration of the shoot, and didn't tell my mom what had happened until the night before we flew back home. She was understandably very upset, and confused as to what she should do. She said something to one of my agents back in NY, and after expressing her concern did her best to put the issue behind us.

That was my first trip to Europe, and I remember the Alitalia flight having designated smoking areas. Ha! Seems like ancient times now. The entire experience of being in Milan was fascinating to me, from all the "*ciao bella!*"'s that I heard throughout my stay, to my amazement at the thinnest-crust pizza I ever did see. I was intrigued by the whole city. The extremely different culture, the sounds, sights, and smells that were so unlike what I was accustomed to. The magnificent Duomo Cathedral and the Camparino in Galleria in the Piazza del Duomo blew me away. Such majestic architecture, such beauty. The Camparino in Galleria by the way is known as *the* bar of the Campari brand and is one of the symbols which is typically associated with Milan, along with the cathedral and the fashion and design industries. And then there was my introduction to bidets. Strange objects—to my American eyes—that seemed so out of place in modern times, but which I learned serve a definite purpose! Which brings me back to the point of this chapter.

The fashion industry, and especially high fashion, is all about glamour—which is heightened sex appeal. I ran across this quote somewhere: "Glamour equals sexual intimidation." And there you have it—the very effective way in which fashion is sold. Models are lovely young women and men who are "translated" by makeup and photography and publicity into images of impossible beauty that others long to emulate or possess. Beautiful clothing after all, which is designed to flatter and show off the body, is a kind of extension of one's sexuality. Sex is naturally part and parcel of the fashion industry. Sex sells. This makes the model a particular magnet for sexual predation. And that's just part of the business, as it is of show business in general. It is up to you to learn how to deal with it.

You will constantly be hit on by both men and women in this industry. The problem arises when the approach and/or the circumstances are inappropriate, constituting a violation. Since women tend to be less predatory by nature than men and since most of the instances I'm referring to involve men, I'm going to focus on men. It can be trying for a young teen to constantly have to deal with aggressive sexual approaches, especially from men they aren't attracted to. You might also be like I had been that day in the dressing room, fifteen years old and a virgin. I was never a prude, far from it. And this isn't a problem when you're over eighteen, but when you're a young teen, it can be very uncomfortable to have to constantly thwart inappropriate advances by much older men, especially when they're your employers. Part of the assumption about you is that because you're sexy in front of the camera, which is your job—and it's also fun to pose and pout for the camera—that you will be this tigress of sexuality off camera as well. Not necessarily. We're talking about teens here, who are still growing up and becoming acquainted with their sexuality, which doesn't mean they want to share it with everyone who comes on to them off camera. It's not that you don't want sex at fourteen, fifteen. It's that you're too young at that age to be having sex with much older people who are in a position to hire and fire you, and to navigate your way emotionally through all that that entails.

I have nothing against a person having sex with whomever they wish, even at the age of fifteen, if it's right for them. But if you're having sex at fifteen, it's generally advisable to do so with someone close to your age. Typically, when a young teen is in a sexual relationship with a man of thirty or forty, there's a troubling imbalance in the power dynamic between them. If he should happen to be her agent or someone else with a position in the industry, the issue goes beyond imbalance to abuse of power. It puts the teen in a very vulnerable position, since it's then not a question of whether or not she wants to sleep with the man, it's a matter of the manipulative pressure that marks the situation. If she decides not to sleep with, e.g., her agent, she could be jeopardizing her career and missing out on a once-in-a-lifetime opportunity. This is clearly not fair to the fifteen-year-old, since it isn't a choice someone of that age is equipped to make.

Something else bears mentioning here. In the fashion industry, very young women are often made to feel that they have to be overtly sexy off camera in order to be able to project sexuality on camera. Well, that's an utter fallacy. Off camera, just be whoever you truly are. Fortunately for me, I never felt the need to constantly call attention to my sexuality in order to feel desirable and was perfectly comfortable with the pace at which I was growing up. Healthy sexual beings don't need to constantly display their sexuality.

So, how to handle sexual inappropriateness when it could cost you your job?

Not easy.

I believe you must follow your instincts about what you can handle emotionally and psychologically as well as physically. Don't ever feel pressure to have sex in order to get work. If you feel completely comfortable having sex with someone in order to secure work, then fine, go for it. Why not? At the end of the day, it all depends on who you are and what you can handle. No one can tell you what's best for you, not even me. Being thrown into lots of sex at an early age in an industry where there are almost no boundaries can be very disturbing for a young teen. So much is coming at you constantly, and fast. You will respond to all advances according to your personality and your degree of stability and self-possession. But if you feel that you are being treated inappropriately, then do your best to calmly say no, and if you must be firm, know that you have every right to be, so that you can stay in your power and say what you need to say, as best you are able. And remember to breathe. If you have never dealt with an uncomfortable confrontational situation, please trust that you can do it. Trust whatever sense of self you may have and do your best to say no if you have to. Do it with humor if the circumstances allow for that—why not? Humor is a wonderful way to defuse a tense situation. "Dance" with the wolves whenever you can. And remember, always process a disturbing episode afterwards by confiding in a trusted friend or mentor. That will help you get a grip on what happened and enable you to move on.

Due to the nature of the fashion business and of human sexuality, you will almost certainly face the kind of situations I'm talking about in this chapter. To the extent you are able, don't let anyone take advantage of you. If you find yourself in an uncomfortable situation, or even worse if you find you're in harm's way, then depending on the degree of discomfort or danger, respond accordingly—again, as best you can. Don't judge yourself if you slip here and there or stumble, stutter, giggle, blush, or cry! Just do the best you can. If a photographer or a client makes advances at you, trust your instinct as to how out of line they are. If the advances are minor but still uncalled for, then try not responding to them at all, or excuse yourself from the room. This can be done subtly, and will let the offending party know that you don't accept being spoken to or treated in an inappropriate manner; and you will have remained in your power without having lost your cool or having said a single word. Actions do speak louder than words. But sometimes the situation calls for words. You will have to gauge when that may be by heeding your instincts. When you must have words with someone who behaves inappropriately with you, try to do it one on one with them, calmly but firmly saying what you must. You may at times need to speak your needs out loud to the person in front of others but, since this can be tricky, choose wisely when to do so and what to say. You don't want to negatively affect your reputation in the business—and you don't have to—by being labeled "difficult," "problematic," "can't work well with others." But that doesn't mean you have to be a doormat. People will respect you more when you are assertive and show that you won't tolerate being treated disrespectfully.

By all means, if you want to flirt with whomever, then flirt away. I've just been addressing those moments in the industry when you might have to deal with sexual impropriety. There are also going to be plenty of men outside of the business who might be just as wolfish as those on the inside. I'm referring to the men you will encounter throughout the world who love to be around models. The wealthy businessmen, the oil barons, et al., are for the most part as interesting and delightful to spend time with—or not—as any other men. But then there are the trashy tycoon types you'll be meeting as well. You can almost smell them a mile away. Now, if you're into the trashy tycoon, then hey, be my guest. But if the general sleaze and BS of their game turns you off as it did me, then just say no. Your way of dealing with them will depend on how aggressively they pursue you. Your call. But don't believe that these slick types can help your career, they can't. If they tell you they can, they're lying, and hopefully you're too smart to fall for that. Most of the time they just want the next pretty young thing on their arm and sunbathing on their yacht for the paparazzi to see. You're disposable to that kind of man, as there's always the next young thing around the corner. And don't put yourself into delicate situations where you can be hurt, maybe even raped. If you haven't met a man through a reliable source and don't know him well enough, then for heaven's sake, use common sense. Don't board his private plane or step aboard his yacht unless you know from a trusted third party that he's okay. Always take a friend with you, never go alone. It's a big world out there full of all kinds of people, including the unsavory sort, so you must be smart and think before you act. If you have never experienced any untrustworthy people in your life, you will have to be extra aware of those slick characters that approach you in and around the industry. Being born and raised in NYC gave me an advantage. I became street smart fast because I had to in such a populous, wired, international town that contains every type of character you can imagine, both good and bad. If that isn't your background, fret not, you will learn quickly just by having to navigate on your own (with or without chaperone) through the industry and various cities.

I'll never forget another model who started in the industry around the same time I did. Her parents, like mine, wanted her to stay in school as much as possible but at the same time didn't want to hold her back from the tremendous opportunity of being a model. Her mother however was one of those women who lived vicariously through her daughter's experiences in the modeling industry: the "stage mom" who had wanted so badly to be in the spotlight herself, but for whatever reason had never gotten there and pushed her daughter to have the kind of experiences she had dreamed of having. The mother was all too happy to accompany her daughter "Patty" on her shoots around the world. Like me, Patty was fourteen when she started modeling. We both stayed in Paris in the models' apartments with our moms at various times in our early to mid-teens. Patty's mom wanted to go out and party with us and our peers almost more than we did, and although she would speak about being careful with whom you go out re: roofies and rape etc., her own behavior was overtly sexual and embarrassing. As you can imagine, this was hard for Patty to take. The adult who should have had her back was behaving like an irresponsible adolescent. Her mom was constantly giving her the following kind of mixed message about men: "Go have sex with him and let him buy you jewelry, but don't trust him!" The poor girl ended up losing herself in wild parties and orgies and became addicted to a mess of drugs. It would have been pretty hard for her not to, getting, as she was, the very opposite of healthy guidance from her own mother. She didn't know whom to trust, nor who she was, and eventually fell victim to the lecherous types that hang around the business. Often they're party promoters, club managers, or guys who just talk a big game and are "friends" with your agent. Mind you, there are many good people in the aforementioned fields, but you have to pick and choose wisely which of them you associate with. If you are unfortunate enough to have similar parenting to Patty's, then seek a grounding source of strength and trust in others around you, perhaps an aunt, sibling, teacher, mentor, friend. Never give up on yourself. If you seek out people who will be there for you, you will find them. For as many louche types as there are around this business, there are plenty of good folks to balance things out. Beginnings like Patty's in the often harsh world of fashion rarely have happy endings. Fortunately however, Patty managed to extricate herself from the downward spiral she had fallen into, and I recently heard that she was happily married with kids.

CHAPTER 6

MANAGING ALL THAT MONEY

YOU ARE GOING TO BE MAKING A lot of money—fast. How do you budget your new lifestyle? What temptations do you avoid? How do you avoid scam artists? How do you save your money? How do you make it grow? If your parent or guardian isn't knowledgeable enough, who do you turn to? Which managers do you trust? How do you invest? The top earning years for a model are short. Don't let all that money slip away.

Modeling is a great opportunity to earn a lot of money in a relatively short period of time. I was brought up in a middle class family and learned the value of not spending all your money at once. I understood from an early age that once money comes in, you spend where you must and on some fun stuff too, but also make sure that a portion of your earnings goes into a savings account of some kind to offset possible financial downturns in your life. I believe trust-fund kids can benefit from this perspective as well, especially in these turbulent economic times. Why on earth anyone would spend all their income at once is beyond me, though apparently some people do. I was lucky that my mother and maternal grandparents instilled in me a practical approach to money. Not everyone has family that does this however, and if you don't, I suggest turning to a trusted family friend or other mentor who can set you in the right direction financially, whether that is a proper mindset or actual **Following page: Seeing double**

85

YVES SAINT LAURENT

Tuxedo jacket (£920) and
trousers (£430), both by Yves
Saint Laurent. Satin sandals
(£300) by Manolo Blahnik.
Bag (£390) by Fior.
For stockists, see page 200

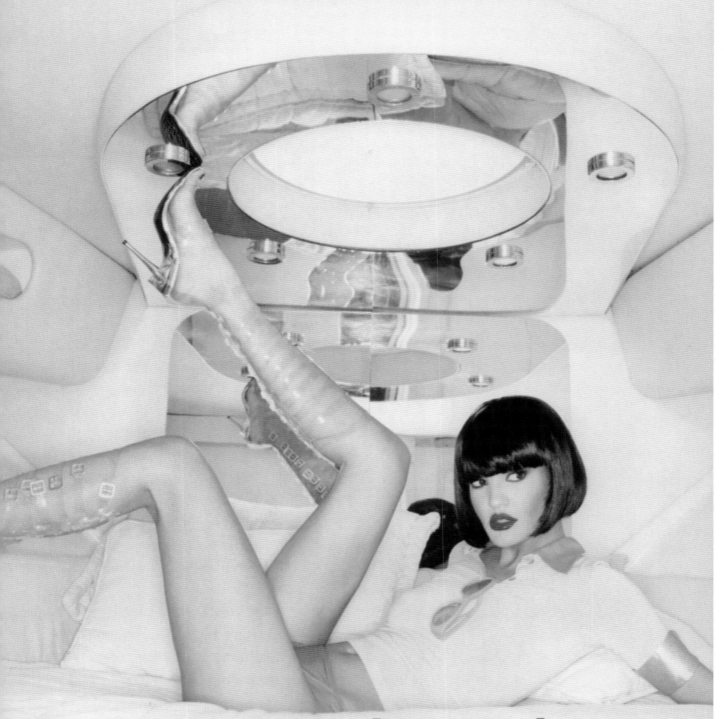

Bond Girl

**She's never shaken or stirred – the Bond girl's
holiday wardrobe is capsule-sized and packed for action**

guidance to good money managers. Sometimes your modeling agents will put you in touch with trustworthy professionals. I met my accountant through Elite, my first modeling agency, and I work with him to this day. You might also get good referrals from associates in the industry. Always get second and, if necessary, even third opinions. And certainly let your gut have a say in the choices you make. If you don't trust the adviser you are interviewing, take note. You may have to ask more in-depth questions or need a second appointment with an investment adviser before you can decide if he or she is right for you. Learn the basics about managing one's money and investing—whether from some of the easy-to-understand books out there or by taking a class or two.

Modeling is a profession that falls under the "self-employed" job category. Even though a model has an agency that gets her jobs, she is still an independent artist who is responsible for paying all her own taxes and obtaining her own health insurance. She is not an employee of the agency that represents her. She doesn't have a built-in 401K (retirement) plan through her job. In fact, it's good to remember that a model "employs" an agency to get *her* work, and starts off paying that agency 20 percent of her earnings for each job. But the agency doesn't work exclusively for the model, it also earns a 20 percent commission from the client. A large portion of your income, assume 40 percent, will be taken for taxes. You pay taxes on your net, not your gross earnings. Be sure to pay your taxes on time to avoid what can amount to very costly penalties. As for health insurance, SAG-AFTRA has an excellent plan that most models are covered by once they've earned a certain amount of money in commercials (or in films). SAG-AFTRA is an American labor union which represents film and television principal and background performers and radio personalities worldwide. If you're a model who doesn't get commercials at all or not very often, you will have to fend for yourself regarding health insurance. Your agency will often be able to refer you to health insurance advisers or companies and then it will be up to you to find a plan that works for you. Be sure to keep your insurance premiums paid up on time.

The way to save your money is to just save it. Discipline yourself to not spend your entire paycheck at once. Remember how short-lived a model's career actually is. I never felt tempted to spend all my earnings at once on, say, a trip around the world and a car. I went on plenty of great vacations, but I always knew there would still be money

GENNY

Silk-chiffon coat (£604) by
Genny. Bikini (£110) by Louis
Feraud. Satin sandals to
order by Jimmy Choo. Trilby
(£90) to order by Stephen
Jones for Nicholas Knightly.
Diamanté choker to order by
Butler & Wilson. Diamanté
earrings (£125) by Sonia
Rykiel. Shopping trolley
(£200) by 31 Février

Rayonnante, en LANVIN
par Claude Montana : robe
marine en soie-ziberline
brodée et tulle.

Rossy de Palma does the Spanish fling with an antique fringed shawl, OPPOSITE PAGE. Another gypsyish trademark—the gaucho hat. By Makins Hats, about $150. THIS PAGE: Not reserved for the high wire—a dress that makes a show of beaded fringe, net, and animal prints with a daring string of jewels for a top. By Atelier Versace. Details, stores, see In This Issue.

© Bruce Weber

Previous two pages: (Left) Gypsy soul in Miami for American Vogue

(Right) I love this photo for British Vogue

in the bank when I returned home. How can I convey the importance of this way of thinking to you? Just consider the employment difficulties your generation faces. Even highly qualified university graduates are having trouble finding work today. It's a tough job market out there, so if you're making money as a model, and you miss out on college because your college-age years are your prime moneymaking years in the fashion industry, then think hard about what you may be qualified to do when the industry is no longer hiring you. That might make you start saving right away! I'm not suggesting you save everything and not live a full, vibrant life. No. But to not save a portion of your earnings would be an irresponsible, foolish way to live.

I was fourteen when I started making money as a model, and although my mother was knowledgeable about saving, she wasn't in the know about investing. Fortunately, she had a close friend who was able to steer me in the right direction financially when I was around eighteen and modeling full time. I've turned to him from time to time since then and have been so grateful for his help. Between this family friend and my accountant, I have been guided in the right direction. For example, I was advised to buy an apartment at a point in my career when it made sense to do so financially, and this has been the smartest economic move I've made. I owned my initial NYC apartment for ten years and made a good profit when I sold it. I've also worked with financial professionals, some good, some bad. Happily, I was always able to fire the bad ones before taking too great a loss. At times, I've invested a portion of my earnings in stocks and bonds—conservatively—when I've been persuaded it was wise to do that. Investing in the market can be very tricky as we've all heard time and again. Don't do it unless you're guided by a knowledgeable, trustworthy professional who has a firm enough grasp on its intricacies and volatility.

Budgeting your lifestyle is important. There are any number of formulas available to achieve this goal. A good general one for how to divvy up your income is to use one third of it for essential living expenses, including taxes; save at least one third; and spend no more than one third on nonessentials. However you choose to manage your finances, remember that discipline doesn't have to be tedious and burdensome, and that structure equals freedom. I have always been the most carefree and happy when I've lined up my ducks properly. The idea of living on the edge of financial ruin is not a place that I ever care to visit, never mind live in. Believe me, having fun on lavish vacations and partying it up is enjoyed best by those who know that the next day's hangover will turn into a happy

Glamour for days . . . French Glamour

Jardin céleste,
par CHRISTIAN DIOR : robe
bustier en taffetas
chiné à imprimé fleuri et
volants en taffetas
plissé ; ceinture brodée.
Maquillage Christian
Dior : Teint actuel Beige
Délicat, poudre Plus
fine Plus qu'Invisible, blush
Final Ardent. Pour les
yeux, palette cinq couleurs
Epices, crayon eye-liner
Noir et mascara Parfait Jais.
Rouge à lèvres Griotte.

sober state due to the fact that there are still plenty of funds left for not only more parties but for living expenses too! Think about it, how enjoyable is it to

constantly find yourself a victim of temptation? Nothing wrong with some good human temptation every now and then, but to live in a constant state of acting upon each and every impulse is not a healthy or sustainable way of living over the long haul. I always thought big picture when I was young, and still do. Ask yourself what the outcome of each and every decision that you make will be not only in the short term but also over the course of your life. It goes fast, this life! And that shouldn't make you feel like you have to be uptight and turn into a miser. No! But be wise. I promise you it's the more attractive option no matter what your age. For example, if your paycheck is $10,000, don't spend it all on one designer bag. Spend some of the $10k on the handbag, then put another portion in the bank or into a smart investment portfolio. You'll most likely be meeting savvy business people including entrepreneurial types in your travels and through your industry connections. You might have the opportunity to make a worthwhile investment in, say, a cool tech company that has come out with a new app, or possibly a restaurant, or commercial real estate. You'll want to have the funds to get in on such an opportunity, yet another benefit to budgeting your income stream. Of course, you shouldn't invest in anything you don't carefully vet beforehand with someone in the know.

Scam artists. How to avoid these creepy players? I've said it before and I'll say it again: Heed your instinct, always. And I'm talking about a healthy gut instinct, not a fearful knee-jerk reaction. You'll know the difference since the former comes from a calm, collected place where you are still breathing, and the latter from a state of panic. Unsavory types can be found everywhere and certainly seem to hang around every corner of the entertainment world, where young people are often their vulnerable prey. When approached by a complete stranger or even someone who introduces himself as a friend of your agent, let's say in a nightclub, for example, take his card and tell him you'll be in touch with him. Keep the contact brief and polite and never feel obliged to give your personal info to him or to make any promises of employing him to act on your behalf regarding your money. If you wish to pursue a contact be sure to vet him through people you trust. If your gut tells you someone who approaches you is unsafe, then just avoid him. Make it a point not to take meetings alone. When you're of legal age, don't sign any document or agree via email to any financial deal offered to you by someone who approaches you without a referral. Remember, it's always best to

get referrals to financial advisers and financial deals from people you trust. It's all right if a financial adviser type approaches you who has been suggested to you or okayed by a trusted acquaintance who is familiar with him. Unfortunately, there are lots of scam artists out there looking to feed off success. Young people are particularly vulnerable to their pitches.

Here are some basics regarding the fees you can make as a model. There are different kinds of modeling jobs and they pay a range of fees. Depending upon a model's status, these fees vary widely.

For instance, editorial jobs can pay as little as $150 a day (and rarely exceed $250 a day). "Editorial" refers to the beautiful photo spreads that change monthly and appear toward the back of a magazine, after all of the advertising pages. These editorial jobs can be for any publication from a small new magazine to *Vogue*. The same editorial rate that is paid for these spreads also applies to most high-fashion magazine covers, including the highly coveted cover of *Vogue*. Hard to believe that being on the cover of *Vogue* doesn't pay the big bucks, but the reality is that a *Vogue* cover is the height of prestige and opens the doors for a model to the big money jobs. Once a model's face is on the cover of *Vogue*, her career opportunities expand exponentially. In contrast, if a model is on the cover of a less prestigious, lower category magazine, she may command quite a bit more money for such a job because it doesn't contribute to the lucrative high-fashion career opportunities.

Advertising campaigns are another category. This is where the opportunity exists for the megabuck contracts. Each advertising campaign is for a specific client, like a clothing design house or a skin care, cosmetic, or perfume line. A contract for an advertising campaign can earn a model anywhere from many thousands to many millions of dollars. The most coveted contracts are for cosmetic, perfume, and skin care brands.

Then there are the bread-and-butter jobs which include bookings for print catalogs, in-store displays and online usage where the pay rate can vary from about a thousand to multiple thousands of dollars a day.

Fashion shows can render highly profitable paychecks as well. A top model under exclusive contract to one designer for one show season can make between $50,000 and $100,000. Generally, fashion shows pay anywhere between $1,000 and $30,000 per show, with $10,000 considered a high rate.

CHAPTER 7

HEALTH, FITNESS, AND NATURAL BEAUTY CARE VS. ANOREXIA, BULIMIA, AND MEDS

WHEN I WAS GROWING UP my mom would allow absolutely no junk food in the house. This included all processed foods, canned foods, fried foods, sodas, candy, even Corn Flakes, because, as she explained it to me, these foods were all poisoned with additives, preservatives, chemicals, and sugar, sugar, sugar. So although that was pretty evident in cereals like Cap'n Crunch, it was not clear to me how Corn Flakes or Rice Krispies fell into the same category of evil. However, those were her house rules, and I had to abide. When I was in the house that is, but outside, away from her health food clutches, I could do whatever I wanted to do, since she would never know, and that I did. I would eat all the pizza, McDonald's burgers, and Dunkin' Donuts I could after school with friends, and then arrive home for dinner. I had always been a skinny kid who could eat whatever I wanted and not put on an ounce of weight, and I had a good appetite. I enjoyed food, that is, yummy-tasting food. Not the gross, "healthy" stuff which tasted like cardboard that my mom made me eat at, say, Souen, the famous macrobiotic restaurant in NYC, when I was nine. Oh how I dreaded hearing that word,

Fronces et lacets
Maillot une-pièce
en polyester et Lycra,
décolleté en V, fines
bretelles, plissé et lacé
sur les côtés (À la Plage).
Mise en beauté Thibault
Vabre pour Lancôme.
Protection et bronzage
parfait avec la ligne à
la mélanine Soleil Passion.
Pour le visage, la Crème
Anti-Rides IP4 et, pour
le corps, le Spray Hydro
Satinant IP4.
Coiffure Guillaume pour
Mod's Hair avec le Spray
Modelant Mod's Hair.

Glamming it up in the south of France for French *Elle*.

"Souen." It was pure misery for me to be dragged through its doors. Today, I love Souen, and will go any time I can, with whomever I can get to go with me. Fortunately, people are more hip today to the importance of eating well for the body's overall well-being and for beauty, and I never really have to drag anybody to Souen, they happily join me. But it was sheer torture to dine there back then, and the only thing I would ever eat from their menu was the shrimp tempura 'cause it was fried, albeit lightly and in the "right" kind of oil at the "right" temperature. I would sit there fuming, arms crossed, occasionally looking at my mommy dearest across the table. I felt that this barbarous imposition of requiring me to eat healthy food was a punishment. Why couldn't I eat the way all my friends and their families ate? "Normal" stuff like cupcakes, and white bread, and soda, and table salt on their salads. To be subjected to carob cake instead of chocolate cake, or whole grain pancakes on a Sunday morning, rather than "normal" pancakes, was an absolute living hell and I was PISSED. My mother didn't make it any easier by being so strict and practically growling at me to "Eat, eat. Stop being a baby, this is good for you. That other stuff is full of poison, poison!" But oh how I wanted that "poison." When I was six, I dreamt that my Candy Land board game would come alive and that I could eat all the sweets in it that I could stuff into my mouth. At school I tried to trade my unappetizing, unwaxed, organic apple at lunch for a Hostess cupcake, to no avail. There was never one kid who wanted my unsalted rice cake with organic butter, instead of their Twinkie. Ugh, utter despair! I remember one quite scarring situation in first grade. It was lunch time, and we were outside, and I opened the packed lunch that my mom had prepared for me, and as I bit into the stiff, thick nine-thousand-grain brown bread, instead of the organic unsalted peanut butter and jelly that I had been told earlier that morning I was getting, I experienced the most foul taste known to man. I spit the nasty mouthful out onto the ground and cried. I was so furious at my mom for this endless torture, this slow death, as I was sure I was being killed little by little by this so-called health food. When I got home later that day and demanded that my mother explain to me what was in that sandwich, she looked in the fridge, and realized she had put tahini on the bread instead of peanut butter. Oh. My. God. How could she?! She felt awful and apologized, but it was too little too late.

Considering all the years of good nutrition that I was forcibly subjected to growing up, as well as the concurrent consumption of junk food as my rebellion against it, it's no wonder I found myself puffy and carrying some extra pounds when I was eighteen and living in Paris as a full-time model. I was told for the first time in my life that I would have to lose weight to continue working at the top level of the business as I was used to. I was aghast.

"Me? Fat?! Me?! – *I* need to watch what I eat? No way." But it was true and I had to face it head on and figure out which foods I would have to avoid in order to lose the extra pounds I had put on, and keep them off. Exercise plays a large part in the quest for a healthy, slim, and fit body. Diet and exercise always work hand in hand. I'll address exercise later on in the chapter, but as for nutrition, it was clear to me at this point that the way my mom had raised me was the right way to go, except a little more tastily! Unfortunately though, I picked up a nasty habit at around the same time: smoking. Smoking a cigarette when you're hungry is an awful but efficacious way to stave off hunger. Plus we all know it makes you feel "cool" to have a cigarette in your hand, especially in Paris, where at any moment, you might find yourself sitting at a café near the Musee Rodin, as you peruse Baudelaire's *Les Fleurs du Mal* while sipping an espresso. While you'll probably pick up a cigarette at some point in your life, I hope you don't feel as if smoking is the only way to keep svelte. It isn't. There are other ways that work even better and keep your body healthy as well as thin, which is the only way to go for long-term sustainability and good looks.

It's important to note that there's a segment of the business which hires plus-size models. In this book I am addressing the mainstream modeling industry, but I want you to know that a size 12+ can also be beautiful and garner a successful modeling career for larger-sized women. And that being healthy comes in more than just the package of a thin body type. It is also worth noting that another, very different category of model, that has more recently begun to gain acceptance, is that of the transgender model.

Anyway, I started to eliminate certain foods from my diet: white bread, sweets, pasta, pizza, and I soon discovered I no longer liked the taste of hamburgers. I stopped eating red meat then and there at eighteen, and I haven't had it since, except on a few rare occasions recently when I've had buffalo burgers. I originally stopped eating red meat because I believed it was fattening me up, and since the burgers I ate were mostly from McDonald's and Burger King, this was true. However, it's important to point out that red meat doesn't make you fat. It all depends on the quality and the fat content of the meat and how frequently you are consuming it. I began to substitute fish, and chicken, skinless at first. Oatmeal and eggs were also part of my diet. Loads of veggies and fruits too. Then I cut out grains altogether, but this is not advisable. You can have whole grains, complex carbs such as brown rice, quinoa, millet, amaranth, etc. I went hard core at first 'cause that's the way I tend to do things, and also because I had to

Larges bretelles et
balconnet, pour le maillot
en coton et lycra,
signé Erès. Sur le visage,
Superior Golden Pro-
tection for the Face SPF8
de la ligne Golden
Beauty d'Helena Rubin-
stein. Fines bretelles
et dos croisé, à droite,
pour le maillot en
lycra, créé par Christian
Dior Boutique. Ma-
quillages Cynthia Walden.
Coiffures Valentin
pour Jean-Louis David.
Réalisation M.-A. Sauvé.

Décolleté carré, pour
le maillot en polyamide
et lycra, signé Erès.
Balconnet et transpa-
rence, à droite, pour le
maillot en lycra et voile
stretch, créé par
Capucine Puerari. Par-
faite protection pour
peaux fragiles : le Lait
Ecran Total Invisible
Résistant à l'eau, Protection Maximale, de Roc.

© Javier Vallhonrat

lose the weight and fast. It wasn't easy in the beginning, especially since I was living in Paris! The land of croissants, *pain au chocolat*, *chausson aux pommes*, *pommes frites*, and the most delightful, sinfully rich chocolate cream pastries you ever did see and taste!

I distinctly remember some of the more difficult times during that initial period of cutting out pastries from my diet, among other foods. As mentioned above, I was living in Paris at the time, I had just graduated from high school, and I was living in a model's apartment in the 1st arrondissement. I'll never forget it. Girls were constantly bringing home baguettes with Nutella spread richly on them, or big, greasy over-stuffed crepes with all sorts of melted goodies inside: tuna and cheese, or nutella and bananas, or ham and cheese. It was hard to resist such mouth-watering delights, especially after a night out at the clubs, when we'd emerge all sweaty, dehydrated from alcohol and cigarettes, and right there outside to greet us were the street vendors, selling their French fast food delights—heaven. But not helpful in keeping with my plan for losing weight. I had to stop eating those fat, juicy crepes as quickly as I had to stop the croissants, and the way I finally stopped consuming the delicious French pastries that are sold in every patisserie, which are on every single Parisian street corner, was to stop in front of a patisserie when I happened to cross in front of one while walking down the street, and inhale the lovely, intoxicating scent that emanated from within. I would literally just stand outside on the street, not caring who was looking at me as though I were a freak, close my eyes and inhale the pastry aroma for as long as I needed to in order to have my fill, and then continue on my way. This cured me of my craving, 'cause during the times that I was standing and inhaling, I would be imagining where on my body the pastries would go if I were to actually indulge the craving and eat them: my hips, my thighs, my stomach, my waist, my butt, etc., and how I would subsequently not be booked for jobs and then what would have been the point of being in Paris in the first place? Either you fit in the clothes or you don't. Period. It's not harsh, it's the business. As with any business, the goal is to sell the product, and in modern culture tall and thin does it. This doesn't mean that you have to starve yourself, becoming anorexic, or turn bulimic. It just means that you must find your own way to eating healthy foods that won't put extra weight on you. I developed my way of coping with this by eating similarly to how I had been raised to eat: a diet full of complex grains and legumes, nuts and raisins, a variety of fruits and vegetables, chicken, turkey, fish, and a limited amount of red meat. I ate tons of Salade Nicoise while living in Paris, and I chose Golden Delicious apples as well as nuts and raisins for snack foods when I needed to keep something to munch on in my bag. Which is not to say I didn't slip up sometimes, that's only human. Or go without eating at times, I did, but I don't recommend doing this because it can really mess with your body later on. Fortunately I'm in good health today, but not everyone is so lucky.

Tan and happy in the Caribbean for Madmoiselle

Another trick is to consume only half of the portion of food on your plate when you're out at restaurants. You'll be taking many of your meals at restaurants, since ours is a social business, and deals are often done over dinner. You can reduce your appetite for heavier foods in a healthy way by starting a meal with hot soup. Eating a lot of vegetables with the meal, including a dark green leafy vegetable, will provide you with many of the nutrients you need and also help cut your appetite for the heavier foods. Sure, I smoked and minimally experimented with diet drugs to curb my appetite, but it's not worth it. It's a gamble that most people lose, especially addictive types.

And what about exercise? It's so important for maintaining a great body. It also makes you feel good, especially *after* a workout. I happen to prefer yoga classes to working out on the machines at the gym. Walking home after a yoga class, I feel like I'm walking on air, because my spine is so straight and aligned, and my feet seem to be just gliding along. Heaven. The right kind of exercise makes me feel so comfortable in my body and good about myself that I can't imagine a life without it. My love of dance got me on the exercise track early in life, and I've rarely gone without some form of exercise for any length of time since. Yoga, like jogging, dancing, or playing a sport, keeps you in shape, sure, but it also clears your mind and just makes you feel better overall. Modeling can be hard, the many pressures that will fall on your shoulders can weigh you down, and one of the greatest forms of release is exercise. I also like Gyrotonics and Pilates as an addition or alternative to the more typical exercise regimes. But whatever way you prefer to work out, do it. Actually gathering yourself together *to go* to the class or gym or court or field is the hardest part. Once there, it all flows.

I've always said it's the combo of a good diet with regular exercise that keeps you looking your best. There is no magic pill, believe me. I've tried a few and they don't work. Nor are they good for you. I'm big on eating well and taking care of myself because it keeps my spirits up as well as my energy, it keeps my skin looking great, and my hair and nails at their best. Clients book you because you are fresh-faced and dewy, with good energy and a great body. Even when the trend swings toward a more down-and-out look or expression, they still want to see a healthy-looking model walk into the studio. The hair and makeup team can always adjust the model's appearance to fit the feel of the shoot. The lighting that the photographer chooses to go with can also greatly affect how

This page: Demure, lacy short-shorts and an eyelet top are a delicate proposition. Shirt, of cotton, by Agnès B., $125. Shorts, of cotton, by Tripp, $20. Opposite: A cropped blouse bares the midriff; lacy hip-huggers reveal what's underneath. Shirt, of viscose georgette, by Ghost at Showroom Seven, $315. Leggings by Tripp, $40. Hat by Eric Javits, $150. Earrings by Erwin Pearl, $25. Hair, these eight pages, by Ray Allington at Nicky Clarke London W.I.; makeup by Diane Kendal for Atlantis Paris. Location courtesy of the Anguilla Department of Tourism and the Casablanca Hotel. For details, stores, see SHOP.

Sea, sand, sun, and SPF. Italian
Marie Claire.

one looks on camera. But coming in healthy and youth-ful-looking will always be in style.

Some people never seem to exercise much, nor eat particularly well, yet they are able to look good and stay in pretty good shape. That's genes for you. But whatever your DNA, when you are happy and thriving your whole body and face seem to be on fire—they look great. Exercise in some form or another is generally a good habit to get into, it certainly will help you last longer in the business. Finding a form of exercise that you're passionate about is the key in my opinion, as I grow easily bored with what for me are uninspiring ways of working out, like spinning classes or the treadmill, *zzzzz*. If you love to do something, chances are you'll do it more frequently and regularly and get better results. I grew up taking dance classes because I love to dance. It was tough to keep up with my dance class schedule as well as my schoolwork, because they were both intense, but I learned how to be disciplined because of that. I believe a love of dance and the strict dance classes I began to take at an early stage in my life formed how I would approach exercise later on, since I learned that I needed to move my body in one form or another in order to feel good and be happy. Physical movement releases endorphins, which make you feel good. I know if I haven't exercised in a while my mood is going to be affected, and as soon as I get my body moving again, I become immedi-ately more relaxed and feel much happier. There are so many reasons to exercise: to stay in shape, to relieve stress and be calm, to feel happy, to keep your skin looking great. Whichever form of it works for you, stick to it. I also appreciate that with yoga, I can do it on my own on the road, a plus in our profession. All you really need is a small amount of bare floor, and if you don't have a mat, then a towel will do. Also, all the traveling that one does in this business starts to get to you after awhile, the long hours on a plane, the jetlag, etc. will make you want to stretch and move your body in some form. Go out for a run, take a swim, do thirty minutes on the elliptical machine, dance it up in a jazz class, or find your Zen spot in a yoga class. Whatever it is that motivates you and brings you joy, begin it and keep at it. It really pays off, believe me. Plus, the more regularly you work out, the more fun foods like pizza, pastries, and French fries you can eat from time to time, because the exercise promotes better absorption of those foods, so they don't end up on your thighs or around your belly as much. Bonus!

And what about beauty products? The most important products out there are water, sleep, meditation, moisturizer, and SPF. If you want to know why I look ten years younger than I am, it's because I get enough sleep, number one. I really need eight hours, which ain't easy all the time, but I operate at my best after a good night's sleep. Getting

Beauty shot for Italian *Marie Claire*

to bed by 11 p.m. is super helpful, as the body has more of a chance to go into restorative in-REM sleep than it would if you get to sleep after midnight. Now I know that this seems like the most BORING suggestion. OMG, how will you party and let loose if you have to be in bed before midnight?! I'm speaking here of the ideal, and clearly when you're a teen and in your twenties, you can subsist on less sleep and still function at your best, but I have always needed a lot of sleep, even when I was a kid, some people just do. So, do what you must, but these are fundamental truths I'm laying out for you, which you can use to your advantage when you need to.

Drinking lots of water is great for your body in so many ways. The more water you down throughout the day, the better your skin will look, and the fewer headaches and digestive problems you will have. Drinking water also helps keep you slim and it flushes away impurities. It can help you avoid hangovers if you drink a glass of water for every equivalent amount of alcohol. Water keeps our internal system flowing, and I can't stress enough how important it is to consume what feels like a sufficient amount of water for you. Now mind you, I don't always meet the criteria that I am laying out for you here. No way. But I do the best I can. The point of advising you to eat well and exercise and wear SPF is not to make you obsess about all this, but rather to let you know there is a good reason why people have been forever saying these same things. They work. Take care of your body, and it will serve you well for a long time. Don't try to be perfect, and when you veer too far from taking good care of yourself, just get back on track when you can. Fall off the "right" way of doing this, and get back up. There is no one right way anyway. No one is perfect, and if you try to eat "perfectly" and take all of your vitamins every day, and exercise four times a week like clockwork, you will surely fail at some point, and that's fine. While there is no perfect way of taking care of oneself, the fact is that eating nutritious foods and exercising go a long way toward helping you to sustain a happy and youthful mind, body, and spirit. And yes, meditation too. This can be as simple as quietly sitting for ten to twenty minutes with your eyes closed while practicing one of the many forms of formal meditation, or taking an exercise class, or spending quality time with people that are meaningful to you, or dancing your butt off at a club. If the body and the spirit are fed, the good looks will follow. Ohm.

When I moved to Paris at eighteen, I had to start exercising regularly since I needed to get in shape, as I mentioned earlier. I found the Paris gyms a comforting and supportive environment for exercise. One reason I suppose was the lovely, lyrical sound of the

French language wafting through the air as I did my leg lunges in the body fitness classes

they offered at the time. I also find that the French generally thrive on organization, which I happen to like as well, because it provides structure to what you're doing, which helps you accomplish your goals. For me, structure equals freedom, and I loved the Paris gyms for their regimented ways of exercising. Those fitness classes covered all the areas of the body in a way that didn't wear you out. In an odd way it relaxed and energized me. Exercising doesn't have to be grueling to be effective, and isn't necessarily better if done on a daily basis. A few times a week is fine. The down time between exercise sessions is as important as the workout itself, so go and enjoy a sauna or a steam, or luxuriate in a massage, or just lay out at the beach. Your body and mind will thank you, because your muscles actually need some days off from exercising to keep in optimal shape.

Talking about steam rooms and saunas, I'll never forget a funny incident that occurred when I was on a job in Germany, in Stuttgart I believe. I was staying in a hotel that had a spa on the top floor, and after a long day on set, I looked forward to indulging myself and zoning out in the steam room. As I was checking in at the spa's front desk, the woman who worked there handed me a locker key, and informed me that the spa was co-ed, and proceeded to say in a very stern voice, "No bathing suits allowed on while in the spa." I thought that I had surely misunderstood her. So I said, "You mean no bathing suits on when in the women's areas . . . ?" which would have been an odd rule to enforce, but hey, different country, different customs. She responded back even more sternly, saying, "No clothing or bathing suits allowed in any areas of the spa at all times." Ha! This is too much, I remembered thinking. She expects gorgeous model me to walk around naked in a massive spa full of strangers, men and women? Is she nuts? All eyes will surely be on me, and how relaxing will that be? I've never been to a nudist colony, but I imagined that I was about to walk right into a German one. I couldn't believe this woman was telling me that I *had* to be naked or I would be asked to leave—hysterical. So I went in, stripped down, and to my surprise none of the men, women, or children of all ages that were around me blinked an eye or stared. It is so interesting to see how different cultures operate, and this is one of the best aspects of being a model. You get to travel and you're exposed to the world, as richly diverse as it is. I had a super relaxing time being naked among a bunch of strangers, which I found to be hilarious. I was actually disappointed that no one looked at me that much. As great-looking and in shape as I was, I couldn't believe it. This "everyone must be naked" rule would never work in America, certainly not at a standard hotel spa! It would be quite the opposite.

madame
FIGARO

JOURS
DE
FRANCE

ANTILLES 18,20 F
CANADA 3,75 $C
COTE-D'IVOIRE 900 CFA
DIVERS AUTRES CFA 1000 CFA
EGYPTE 12 EP
ESPAGNE 375 PES
GRANDE-BRETAGNE 1,75 L
GRÈCE 450 DRC
HOLLANDE 6 FL
ITALIE 5000 LIT
MAROC 15 DH
PORTUGAL 300 ESC
RÉUNION 18,20 F
SÉNÉGAL 850 CFA
SUISSE 4,20 FS
TAHITI 1035 FCFP
TUNISIE 1300 MIL
NEW YORK 3,25 $

300 PAGES
SPECIALMODE

T 5919 - 406 -

© Tyen

Great cover shot for *Madame Figaro*

A note about the model having to keep sufficiently thin to fit the sample-size clothes and display them to maximum effect: On the one hand, this is simply a requirement of the job. On the other hand, when dealing with teenagers, who are still growing, they have food cravings that are not easy to subdue. But there doesn't have to be a "freak out" mentality associated with being thin, since it doesn't have to be seen as a punishment. It's very helpful when agencies pay attention to this issue and provide the young models with the support they need. This should include counseling about diet, so they can maintain optimum weight for the business and at the same time address their cravings in a healthy way. Fortunately, agencies are increasingly dealing with this issue. Let's remember, if a model isn't thin enough to fit into the clothes, she'll soon enough be rejected. Severe competition and the risk of rejection are constants in the entertainment industries. The young model can use all the help she can get to avoid or soften what can feel like very harsh blows.

Finally, here are:

CLAUDIA'S MUST-HAVES ON THE GO

NUTRITION		BEAUTY		EXERCISE	
WATER		SPF		A MEDITATION PRACTICE	
FRUIT		LOTION		10–20 MINS. FOR EXERCISE	
NUTS, RAISINS/ DRIED FRUIT		LIP BALM/ LIPSTICK		EXERCISE BAND/ TOOL	
A HEALTHY PROTEIN BAR		HAIRBAND		EXERCISE MAT OR TOWEL	
VEGGIE CHIPS		MASCARA			
VITAMINS C & B12		COVER STICK			

CHAPTER 8

SEX, DRUGS, AND ROCK 'N' ROLL

ENTICING ... NAUGHTY ... WILD! ... These are all words that come to mind when I see this chapter heading. Some rock 'n' rollers go into a band just for the opportunity to have sex with as many models as they can. 'Tis true. I've heard it being said. Of course the goal of having sex with models applies to finance guys, actors, lawyers, and sports stars as well, but I'm focusing on rock stars here. They're so alluring aren't they? So sexy. And they want *you*. What fun! Yes, models and rock stars have been coupling forever. And why not? They look great together for one, and both are used to being told that they're beautiful and "a god/goddess" by everyone they come across wherever they go. Success attracts success, winner attracts winner. They have similar lifestyles and are used to having handlers, agents, and managers who tell them what to do and where they'll need to be and when. They're very much drawn to each other, as they mirror one another in a lot of ways. And they're both sexy as hell.

When I was about nineteen or twenty, I remember being with a friend at a rock concert. The band was huge at the time. It was a great show and we were thoroughly enjoying ourselves as we danced and sang along with the band from our front row seats. As the last song came to an end, and the band took their bows, the lead singer

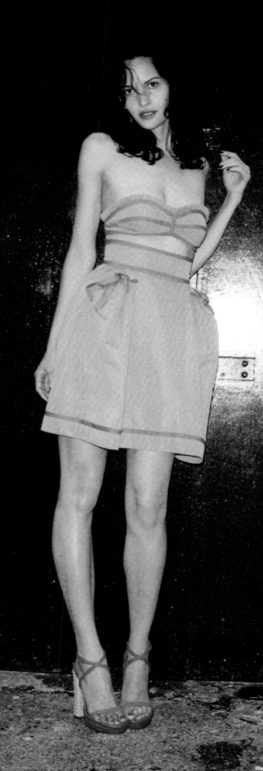

Claudia

Claudia wears bra, skirt
and shoes all by YVES
SAINT LAURENT
cruise 2011; diamond
hoop earrings by DAVID
MORRIS

Sexy in Saint Laurent for *Love* magazine looked out, recognized us as we were cheering them on, and signaled for us to come backstage. Fun! We soon found ourselves amidst many other celebs and their handlers. And a lot of booze. We were introduced to the rest of the band, and I hit it off immediately with the cute bass player. I remember that he was shorter than me, which normally wasn't my thing, but our chemistry was so electric that his height was the last thing on my mind. Before I knew it, we were making out in a car on the way to their hotel where the party was going to continue in their master suite.

At many of these kinds of parties, but as it happened not at this particular one, a whole lot of everything tends to go on, all the sex, drugs, and rock 'n' roll you can imagine. The fact is that most people working in the highly stimulating world of youth, beauty, money, and excitement that is the world of fashion and other entertainment industries, are bound to have a greater number and variety of sensual experiences than most people. This is how it has been since the beginning of time wherever those factors exist in combination.

I ended up dating this bass player for the next few months whenever he was in town. As much as I enjoyed being with him, I wasn't sure that I wanted to establish a committed relationship with him. After all, I was young and not sure I was ready to settle down. Somehow, this made me feel like a "bad" girl. For a perennial "good" girl, that was a lovely feeling. A memorable moment that stands out from our affair was when his band played on *Saturday Night Live*, which I believe I had been more excited about than he had been. He gave me my pass, and I arrived at the show all dolled up with these great high heel black leather boots on that were a favorite of mine back then. I took my seat, delighted that I was going to be an audience member for a live taping of one of the most iconic New York TV shows ever. The lights went down and the show began. I don't at all remember who the host was that night. All I remember was that when the band went on, I was thrilled. I had a secret that no other audience member was in on, which was that I was with the band. Just one more aspect of being part of a privileged inner circle that relatively few people have access to. The fact is, when you're a beautiful girl, particularly if you're a model, you automatically have entrée to the most desirable circles. Your presence is wanted everywhere and people love to lavish attention as well as gifts on you. You get used to being treated *like* a rock star, and it's easy to let this go to your head. Of course, if you're actually dating a rock star, and he's the one getting more of the attention, then you are suddenly relegated to being the arm candy, even if people know who you

Following page: It's all about the boots. Russian *Vogue*.

are. You're still "the model so-and-so rock star is dating."
This is humbling for the massive ego that can understand-
ably develop as a byproduct of supermodeldom. The band played well on SNL, and I had
a blast at the after-party with many other celebrities. I remember my guy not being happy
with how his performance had gone earlier for the show, and he was so down about it,
I didn't know what else to tell him other than how great he had done. I was surprised at
how hard he was being on himself. Whatever he felt was "off" about his performance and/
or the band's job that night on the whole wasn't evident at all to me or to the audience,
judging by the wild applause afterwards. I realized how much pressure even successful performers like him put on themselves, and how unnecessary I found it to be. How truly futile
that is. Although unaware of it at the time, I later realized this applied to me as well. And
if you become a successful model, it will also apply to you.

Another time he and I had been out and about together during our liaison was after
the band played a set for a prestigious awards show in New York. I had that same feeling
of exhilaration as I watched him play from my seat. After the show, we went over to a
private party that Ron Wood of The Rolling Stones was throwing in his hotel suite. There
were plenty of things flowing: booze and other substances, music, laughter, and just plain
fun. It was delightful for me to meet such a legend as Ron Wood. He was easygoing and
nice, and he asked if he could draw me. Why on earth would I have said no? So I posed
for him, and he drew my portrait. He is quite a good artist as well as a great musician, and
I kick myself to this day for not asking him to give me that signed portrait of myself. When
these kinds of parties really get going, you never know when tempers will flare. Or when
somebody's wife who is present might decide that she wants all the mistresses present
to leave. (No, I'm not referring to Ron Wood.) But don't judge too swiftly here. Some
celebrities (like some other men) are in open relationships with their wives. And what
about sleeping with men who are in relationships? I'm not about to say that's right. No. But
sometimes life presents you with ambiguous situations where you have to consider what
decisions you can live with at the end of the day. Based on the facts that you are presented
with, how much harm are you causing yourself or others? And what consequences can
you live with? Life is full of experiences, and chances and choices. I don't promulgate ram-
pant casual sex, nor do I believe in sleeping with a man who is in a committed relationship
with another woman. However, sometimes these circumstances are not fixed, and one
must decide in each and every instance, what one should or shouldn't do.

A note regarding the question of sexual promiscuity: Some people seem to be promiscuous by nature. It's

OUT OF AFRICA

Left: gold resin earrings (from £45) by Dinosaur Designs. Brass and paste pearl neckpiece (£465); brass and silver-coloured breastplate (£750), both by Slim Barrett. Hand-painted silk chiffon scarf (£520) by Joe Casely-Hayford. Right, on both arms: two painted gold-coloured wooden elasticated bracelets (£9.95 each) to order by Etnika. Gilt spiral cuffs (from £70) by Van der Straeten. 24-carat gold-plated on sterling silver hammered cuffs (from £184) from a selection by Crowther Sieff. Yellow metal bra pendant breastplate (£1,185) by Ashanti. Photographer Enrique Badulescu/ Stylist Cathy Dixon/ Hair Guido for Toni & Guy/Make-up Miranda Joyce for Chanel/Model Claudia Mason. For ELLE's Shopping Guide, see page 130

© Enrique Badulescu

CHANEL

Tweed jacket (£2,630 for
suit) by Chanel. Swimsuit
(£16.99) by Knickerbox.
Bag to order by Versace

Creating a role: express yourself! British *Elle*.

a matter of how much promiscuity one can handle, since again, there can be consequences, professional or otherwise. Go out and have fun by all means. Live your life to the fullest, but heed your inner voice and proceed according to who you are. Everyone is different, so what's right for one might not be right for another. Trust yourself, you can always change your mind if you need to. And let no one ever make you feel as though they own your body. You are indeed the sole owner of yourself.

In any case, STDs are out there, and if you are going to have sex with someone you hardly know, whoever he might be, be wise. Use a condom. It's your health, and possibly your life, on the line. The percentage rates of STDs are on the rise all over the globe. So listen to your gut, that strong voice that guides you. It will not lead you astray. Don't ever feel that you have to give your body to anyone, or have unprotected sex, in order to be liked, to generate income, or to be loved. It just doesn't work in the long run. Trust yourself, and be brave enough to walk away when you must. If it's a true situation, then it will still be there for you in the end. Hey, I'm not trying to be a party pooper. Have a blast! Just be aware.

I also remember how we supermodels were treated like rock stars, in Milan especially, at the height of the supermodel era. We each had a driver, aka bodyguard, who would inevitably be a cute Italian playboy-type and everywhere we went, fans would beg us for our autographs, especially outside the Fiera where the fashion shows were held in Milan. There were plenty of affairs going on between models and drivers, and when the boyfriends would come to town, the drivers would assume their best behavior. I was engaged at the time to a South American photographer who didn't let me out of his sight. Although he had nothing to worry about, he never trusted any of my drivers, and would grill me after he had met them. I also recall hanging out with a sports star in the hotel where we all stayed in Milan. He was dating one of the other supermodels, and threesomes were part of their lifestyle together. I was invited into them, but it just wasn't my thing. I tell you this to make the point again: nothing wrong either way, just do what *you* want to do and don't do what you don't want to do no matter who is suggesting it.

And what about drugs . . . ? Yes, that aspect of the business. We have to talk about it, although, like the need for protected sex, it's uncomfortable to speak about the potential downside of using drugs. Why? Because sex and drugs are "cool." Sex sells, and in no greater way than in the fashion industry. Sex is "hip," sex is "youth," sex is what we all want to be having. So no one wants to talk about the potentially harmful aspects of sex.

Sex is part of the culture, part of being human. It not only *feels* good, but it *is* good for you. But then there's the flip side where we enter into the dark waters of STDs etc., which I mentioned above. With drugs, they often are fun and drug experimentation is okay up to a point, but you have to know your point. If you have an addictive or unstable personality, there can be pretty bad consequences. So think before you gamble. Are you really trying that drug because you're genuinely curious about it and feel safe in your environment? Which can possibly be okay depending on what kind of drug it is. Or, are you feeling pressured by those around you to "be cool," and "just go with it, it's no biggie and it'll make you feel better" kind of thing . . . ? Whether you are modeling in front of the still camera, moving camera, or walking the catwalk, you are getting paid to look your best and be alert. So remember, you won't last long on set if you're strung out. They will fire you *tout de suite* (right away), and there are rarely exceptions to that rule.

In terms of addiction, I was lucky, since I don't have an addictive personality. I experimented here and there, but I always knew when to stop. My experimentation was infrequent, and I enjoyed what there was to enjoy, and then I stopped experimenting since I found it to be trifling, unproductive, and not much fun at all. I'd rather be awake and alive in my sober mental state, and enjoy natural highs and lows. The "everything is perfect" state that drugs induce in one is futile for me, since nothing is perfect, and I'm reminded of this when I'm on a drug. I feel safer and grounded and free in my sober consciousness, and unsafe and flailing when on a drug.

I remember being on my first-ever modeling job for a leading fashion magazine of the time. They had booked me for an editorial spread, and to my delight they put me on the cover as well. The actual shoot had about four models including myself, and I was the youngest at fourteen years old. I was shy and uninitiated in the ways of drugs. I had puffed on a cigarette once before at age nine until I gagged, and I once had a toke of a joint at age twelve, but that had been it. So, I was intimidated and uncomfortable when I was offered a joint in the location van on set. We had been shooting out at Jones Beach (New York). It was early evening and the last picture had just been taken moments before, so the crew was winding down, which is natural post-shoot. Everyone was relaxing and looking forward to whatever their evening plans would be once we arrived back to the city. Music was playing, the sun was setting, and as the assistant stylists and the photo assistants were putting away their gear, a joint was lit and passed around to those of us in the van. This is no big deal, and shouldn't be cause for alarm,

Making an entrance . . . in the Caribbean for *Vogue*

Following two page spread:
Finding shade from the heat—British *Vogue*

THE BEST EVENING WEAR WORKS WITH S-SHAPES, FOLLOWING THE LINES OF THE BODY AND ACCENTUATED BY A CURVING FISHTAIL ON JASPER CONRAN'S NAVY JERSEY DRESS, PART OF WHAT HE CALLS HIS "PULL-ON-AND-YOU'RE-DONE APPROACH TO GLAMOUR", *OPPOSITE*, £306. PURPLE GLASS AND SILVER BEAD BELT, FROM £260. BOTH AT SELFRIDGES

BODY SHAPE IS IMPORTANT — EVEN WHEN IT DOESN'T DEFINE THE SILHOUETTE — HAZILY VISIBLE THROUGH SHEER FABRICS. SILK ORGANZA TUNIC, *THIS PAGE*, SLIT UP EACH SIDE, £280, OVER WASHED-SILK ORGANZA FLARED TROUSERS, FROM £270. ALL BY CALVIN KLEIN, AT HARVEY NICHOLS. HAIR: PASCAL DANGIN FOR JAM. MAKE-UP: GLENN MARZIALI FOR TRISH MCEVOY, NYC. FASHION EDITOR: MADELEINE CHRISTIE

Only a teeny bit as it used to be, this season's bikini has two key changes – a curve-cut bottom and a top that doubles as a bra: white cotton underwired bikini top with matching briefs, by Eres, £110, at Harvey Nichols; Night Owls.

Beauty note: when skin looks this good don't spoil it with too much sun and not enough moisture. Ambre Solaire's new UV Sport range comes in SPF4, 8 and 16 and its water-resistant, sweat-resistant formula moisturises while it protects. But don't forget to apply generous dollops of Ambre Solaire Instant Relief After Sun with jojoba oil and vitamin E

The ELLE team
flew with KLM
and stayed with
Georgine y Carlos
Morales, PO Box
150, Bungalows
Los Delfines,
Puerto Escondido,
Oaxaca, Mexico,
tel 010 52 958 2
04 67. For
reservations, contact
Cathy Matos,
Mexican Tours, 61
High Street, Barnet,
Herts EN5 5UR,
tel 081-440 7830

The backdrop falls. British *Elle*.

but I was nervous, since I didn't want any, and it made me feel unsafe. Note: with the current age restrictions on models in the fashion industry, these kinds of things aren't happening as much now. One group in particular, The Model Alliance (MA), mentioned in an earlier chapter, which is a not-for-profit labor group for models working in the American fashion industry, seeks to improve the American modeling industry by empowering models themselves. No one pressured me into it back then, but there was definitely a feeling of "if you're cool, then you take a drag of it." Remember, I was fourteen, and coolness and being cool is at the forefront of one's life at that age; you never want to be seen as uncool. So I took some people's reactions to me, including the photographers, of "Come on, try, there's no harm . . . lighten up" as me being uncool and rigid. I felt awful, and I just wanted to be as far away from this scene as possible in that moment.

Look, you're going to have sex and (most likely) experiment with drugs. I'm just reminding you that there's plenty of sex to be had without losing yourself. And with drugs, if you're going to experiment, be wise.

CHAPTER 9

COLLEGE AND LIFE AFTER MODELING. BE PREPARED.

MY PARENTS DISPLAYED GREAT wisdom regarding decisions that had to be made around my modeling career at its inception. Although they were both excited and delighted for me that such a great opportunity had seemingly fallen upon me from the sky, they were not unreservedly impressed by the glitz and glam of it all. They understood that the opportunity did not guarantee a career and would come at a cost because it posed difficult questions that you too will face: Do you leave school and complete your high school education by correspondence? Do you stay in school and miss out on a once-in-a-lifetime opportunity? Do you transfer to a school that allows time off from regular school hours to give students time for their professional work as well as their schoolwork? What to do? And how about when you and your parents don't agree? What then? Up until what age should an adolescent be required to follow parental guidance . . . sixteen? Eighteen? I feel that eighteen is the time when a young woman or man can leave formal education behind, if and only if they have already been working and are on a professional track, as is often the case with models, actors, and athletes. The length of a model's career is very similar

MODERN TIMES

With fabrics borrowed from his menswear
collection and a few new
feminine accessories, Calvin Klein
creates a city wardrobe for fall
that's "soft and modern"

Girl power—American *Vogue* to that of a professional athlete's. There is a short span of time when she will be at her highest earning capacity, and that time period is usually from fifteen to thirty years of age IF she is lucky and is blessed with an enduring career that lasts more than a season or two. The average career span of a professional athlete is 3.5–5.5 years compared to the average length of a model's career, which is four years. The aim is not just to be the hot face of the moment, only to fizzle out by the following year. No, you want to have as long a career as you can, which does take strategic planning on the part of your agents, but also depends on your ability to hold your own as a professional in this particular business world. Careers, like mine, can and do last well past thirty. But those are not typical cases. Of course fate plays a role in it too. For no matter how perfectly your agent is guiding your career, or how well brought up you are, inhabiting the highest sense of self-esteem etc., the stars must still align in your favor. It's an unpredictable business, where it doesn't matter how smart you are or how professional, nor how perfectly photogenic you might be, and expressively free in front of the camera. If your look is not what happens to be au courant in the fashion industry, then you just might not have a career. If my look wasn't hot and of the moment when I was discovered, I might not have had the phenomenal career I have had. The same goes for names such as Cindy Crawford, Kate Moss, Gisele Bundchen, and the current IT girl Gigi Hadid.

Since there's so much that is out of your hands, you must trust your instinct and go after what you want as best you can. Staying in school up until eighteen won't negatively affect your career too much, and besides, you need at least a high school diploma to move forward in the world after you leave modeling behind. Three of my agents took my mother, my father, and me out to dinner when I was fourteen, in order to persuade my parents to let me leave high school, get my GED, and become the star they saw my career trajectory heading toward. It was a very glamorous evening for me, as we were wined and dined in what for me was a fancy restaurant. I felt so special! Glamour and fame are such temptresses. I think my three agents were used to parents who were so awestruck by what was being dangled in front of them, that they would just say yes to anything that was handed to them by the powers that be in the industry. My parents were New York City born and raised. They were educated, intelligent, and sophisticated. As happy as they were for this amazing opportunity that was presented to their daughter, they were also aware of the pitfalls. They wanted to support me in what I wanted to do, but they had no intention

Following two page spread: **The gypsies: me with Gary Cherone and Nuno Bettencourt of Extreme; Rossy de Palma and friends for *Vogue***

soul

A wild streak of femininity runs through fashion now as designers let loose with sexy silhouettes, flamboyant flounces, and a clash of brilliant prints. Bringing the free-spirited mood to life: photographer Bruce Weber and a few key players—model Claudia Mason, musicians Nuno Bettencourt and Gary Cherone from Extreme, and Spanish actress Rossy de Palma

The nomad's existence is an extended-family trip. While the group cavorts in the open air, Claudia looks ahead in a midriff-tied plaid shirt and a skirt that's a feverish construction of tiered floral patterns. Shirt by Ralph Lauren Classics. Silk skirt by Christian Lacroix. The flower-strewn children are swathed in wrap tops and miniskirts by Complice. Caravan designed by Dimitri Levas. Details, stores, see In This Issue.

Fashion Editor: Grace Coddington

109

of letting me leave high school to get a GED. Fortunately, neither did I wish to at heart, although I was more seduced

by the sheer thrill of my incredible induction into the business and fantasized about what it would be like to leave school and be a full-time glamorous star. At the same time, I instinctively knew that I needed to stay in a school environment in order to feel safe. Yes, safe. That is a heavy word to use, but it is the word that comes to mind when recalling what my feelings had been at the time. By no means did I want to let this fairytale opportunity pass me by, not by any stretch of the imagination. However, I was fourteen. Fourteen! And I enjoyed being fourteen, and I had no desire to be twenty-two, or eighteen for that matter at that moment in my life. My world of high school, friends, ballet class, and boys were just fine for me thank you. The world of fashion, as exciting as it seemed thus far, was also an alien world of adults, sex, money, and uncertainty. I instinctively knew that I was not ready to jump into it full time at fourteen, and leave myself behind in the process. I was a slow bloomer, and fortunately my parents respected my needs and didn't pressure me to leave school. In fact, my dad insisted on me not only staying in high school, but getting into college as well. I didn't have to go he said, but I had to get in. He said I'd thank him later. And I sure have.

What one can learn by living and traveling around the world is a higher education of its own kind. However, I still get boastful today when I talk about the three top-tier colleges that accepted me when I was eighteen. I gained a strong sense of myself by going through the college application process as a high school senior, and the fact that I was accepted into Bowdoin, Connecticut College, and Sarah Lawrence gave me a sense of myself beyond that of being a fashion model. It gave me the validation that I was intelligent enough to do anything I wanted to do. Now you don't need a college acceptance letter to feel this way about yourself, but why not give yourself the opportunity of applying to colleges if it doesn't negatively affect your modeling career time-wise.

I distinctly remember getting around New England with my parents for the college interview process. It was exciting to see the beautiful campuses of the great liberal arts schools in that region. Even though I knew I would most likely not be attending college at the usual time in life right after high school because I was a model in high demand, it was tremendously gratifying to be interviewing for that. I applied to five schools in the Northeastern states, and being accepted into three gave me an incredible sense of accomplishment. The fact that Bowdoin is Mini Ivy League and, as I recall, I was the first student in their admissions history they allowed to twice defer freshman year, gave me an even greater sense of achievement.

Hearts on fire,
left: red leather
waistcoat
with tassels and
heart motifs
(£318); crossover
top (£138), both
by Moschino Cheap
& Chic. Wool/
poplin/cowhide-
back trousers
(£207) to order by
John Galliano.
Red and gilt hoop
earrings (from
£99) from a
selection by
Moschino Bijoux.
24-carat gold-
plated pendants,
round (£85),
heart-shaped, just
seen, (£110),
both by Robert Lee
Morris for
Van Peterson

I had been a reader in high school and was considered a good student. When I became a model, I didn't want to feel that part of me was disappearing. I was a smart girl too, not just a model. Somehow I needed to hold fast to this conviction because modeling wasn't fully satisfying for me, even though I enjoyed it. But I knew it was the current path to follow and that I was very lucky to have the kind of modeling career I had. These were my college years, and there was a part of me that knew I was missing out on a formal education at any one of the great colleges I had gotten into. I needed to justify to myself that I was intelligent, more so than some of the models I encountered who barely had a high school education and showed very little interest in anything outside of fashion, never mind getting into college. And so I prided myself on reading great literature and seeing classic exhibits at the museums in Paris and London, and reading the newspaper whenever I could. I had to be immersed in the world at large as well as in the bubble of modeling, which not only was all-consuming and stifling at worst, but a bit too mindless for me to thrive on exclusively year after year after year.

You can always attend college later on when your modeling career starts to slow down, typically in your late twenties. I have not attended college to date, but I would certainly take college courses if I felt the need and desire to get a degree in a particular field for work purposes. There are many models who have gone back to school post-modeling, or taken courses during their careers via correspondence or night classes. Anything is possible once you make your mind up about your long-term goals. I had always viewed myself as a performing artist. I was convinced that my next career was going to be an acting career. Always the serious planner, I decided to go to theatre school in New York City, since I wanted to be taken seriously as an actor and not thought of as just another cover girl turned silver screen babe. I envisioned myself in Woody Allen films and Shakespeare plays as well as big Hollywood blockbusters. After attending the renowned HB Studio and various independent acting classes with master teachers in New York City, I felt I was ready to move to Los Angeles and focus full-time on acting. I was in my late twenties at the time, and apart from the fact that I was a high-fashion model-type beauty, I was also 5'11.5"—way taller than most female thespians; I really stuck out and not in a helpful way for film roles. Hollywood casting directors didn't know what to do with me. And all my earlier classical theater training didn't account for much in La La Land where in their eyes I was "too pretty" for the more substantive roles that I was capable of playing. I acted here and there in film, TV, and theatre and I produced film and theatre as well which was highly satisfying. Eventually, I got frustrated with the system and moved back to New York.

So I never saw college as a need in my life. Remember, I was a top model. Through good financial planning and investing (see Chapter 6), I was able to pursue an acting career for some time without having to work at anything else. Although modeling was still very much happening for me, I mostly withdrew from it during that period to give my acting career as much of a chance as possible. Not everyone can do that. If I hadn't wanted to be an actor, I might have taken college courses instead of acting classes, but at the time I was set on Hollywood. The important thing to remember is that you can use modeling as a stepping stone to the rest of your life. Consider what you may want to do when your modeling career has ended. Use the connections you make from the industry to facilitate your move into your next career. I was introduced to my current entertainment agent by one of my modeling agents in London. Keep up with the contacts you make in this business, since they're often connected to people in other industries.

What is life after modeling? How do you cope with being "old" at thirty? What do you do? How do you not fall apart when you're not the cute young thing any longer? Look, we live in a youth-oriented culture. Teens and twenty-somethings are the age groups that provide most of the images used in advertising to sell almost everything from perfume to cars. Even so, I imagine it feels pretty crappy to suddenly discover that you're not as hirable once you hit thirty as you had been a decade before even though you still look great. Yet this is the reality for most models as well as for most women in the entertainment world generally. Women in other industries are more likely to face this issue ten years later. It can be scary to experience the instability of your career, even though the continuation of the work was always uncertain. This is the nature of most careers in showbiz. But if you're a child when you start and you're in high demand, you're not at all aware of this reality.

Once you get older and you start getting fewer and fewer bookings, you can suddenly be hit with the awful feeling of "Now what?" You might start to question who you are and how wise your decisions along the way have been. You might tell yourself that you couldn't have done it any differently since the industry had grabbed you up, and finding the time for anything else such as formal education hadn't been possible. This might be true, but it doesn't solve the current problem of what to do with the rest of your life. Modeling ill-prepares you for any 9–5 type of work, that's for sure. Unless that's what you're naturally inclined to. You might be ready to settle down and start a family and also figure out what your next career will be. And as I mentioned earlier, going back to school for a specific profession is always an option. I would say it

Following page: Strumming a guitar in Washington Square Park, NYC— *Mademoiselle*

GRUNGE

Popularized by the
Seattle music scene,
this down-and-dirty
style has hit
the mainstream

THE SOUND AND THE FURY

© Walter Chin

Herrlich feminin

Nicht der flache Slipper, sondern der hochhackige Pumps oder gar die Sandalette geben dem klassischen Hosenanzug ein neues Image. <u>Linke Seite:</u> einfach gut – der strenge Anzug aus Schurwolle mit weißseidener Jabotbluse. Dazu hochhackige Pumps mit Knöchelspange. Alles von Jil Sander. <u>Diese Seite:</u> Modern Dandy in Naturseide – Anzug mit figurnah geschnittenem Jackett, schmaler Hose und passender Weste. Darunter eine gepunktete Organzabluse mit Manschettenknöpfen in Herzform. Alles von Complice. Die Stoffsandaletten mit Straßbroschen sind von Sidonie Larizzi.

© Pamela Hanson

325

depends on where you are financially once your modeling career starts to die down and how much you want to continue working even if you have made enough money not to have to be concerned about that.

What about the emotionally difficult issue of having been the hottest thing on the planet for a number of years, to finding yourself "past your prime"? This can drive anyone to self-medicate via a variety of negative outlets, and unfortunately that happens a lot. But you can also decide to discover who you are at this juncture in your life, by possibly turning to traditional therapy and/or meditation and other spiritual practices for guidance and reorientation. You're lucky if you have a solid family and community of friends. Hold onto the good people you know, whether familial or not, and however few in number they may be. The support of people who care is the best balm for the soul. Redefining oneself career-wise at thirty isn't normally what people go through, since with most trades and professions there's a progressive growth process for the long haul of a person's working life. Modeling is short-lived, so you must deal with starting a new career when most people in other vocations are getting promotions. Instead of viewing this as defeat, view it as opportunity. Not easy, no, but this is why you want to use the wonderful contacts you've made in the relatively short time period of your career to help facilitate your next one, whatever it might be. Since you are older now, you might also view no longer being the cute young thing as a liberation into an appreciation of the joys and benefits of being a grown-up woman.

CHAPTER 10

BRANDING

IN "WILDE IN AMERICA," a new biography of Oscar Wilde, the flamboyant, brilliantly talented 19th-century Irish playwright, author David M. Friedman makes the point that Wilde was one of the first people to grasp that celebrity could come before achievement. "Fame would *launch* Wilde's career," he says, "not *cap* it."

That's exactly what the hot phenomenon of branding is about today, becoming famous—whether or not one has achieved or will ever achieve anything of substance. While most people who successfully brand themselves nowadays do so after a lot of accomplishment, many others who succeed at becoming a brand have accomplished very little, if anything.

While an entertainer, like certain TV personalities, who makes a living in front of the camera doesn't have to be talented to have a following today as opposed to in the past, care has to be taken with performers who rise too fast, because they can also fall fast when they don't have much substance to begin with.

In the '90s, top models made megabucks and were featured on the covers of the leading fashion publications. Then things shifted. For one thing the online world had arrived,

Following two pages: (Left) In Monaco with Kristen McMenamy for Fendi campaign

(Right) Christian Lacroix campaign

FENDI

720 FIFTH AVENUE
NEW YORK

BAL HARBOUR   HOUSTON   WASHINGTON D.C.

ALSO AVAILABLE AT NEIMAN MARCUS

© Karl Lagerfeld

MOD. 7391

CHRISTIAN LACROIX

Lunettes

© Tyen

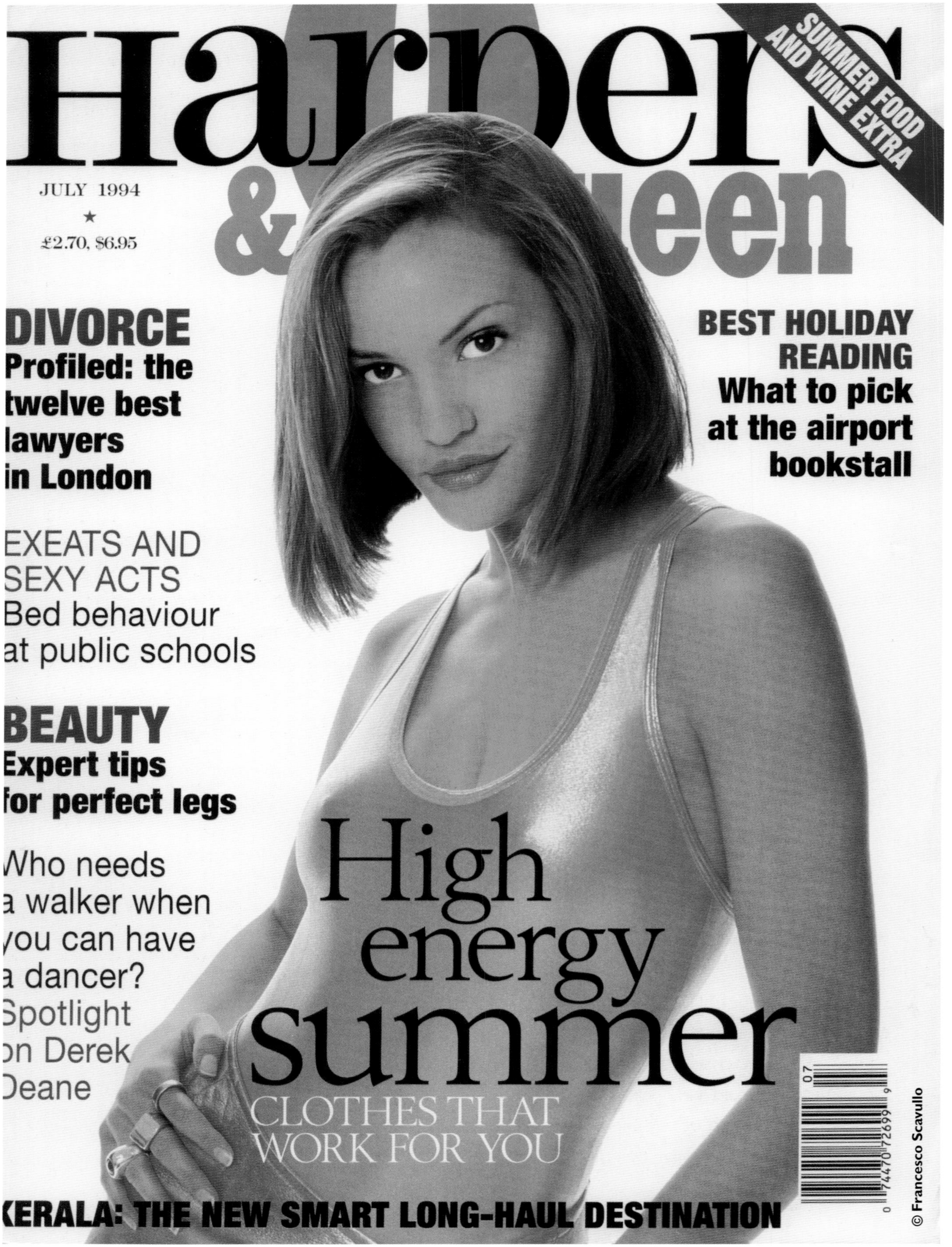

Harpers & Queen
SUMMER FOOD AND WINE EXTRA
JULY 1994
★
£2.70, $6.95
DIVORCE
Profiled: the twelve best lawyers in London
BEST HOLIDAY READING
What to pick at the airport bookstall
EXEATS AND SEXY ACTS
Bed behaviour at public schools
BEAUTY
Expert tips for perfect legs
Who needs a walker when you can have a dancer? Spotlight on Derek Deane
High energy summer
CLOTHES THAT WORK FOR YOU
KERALA: THE NEW SMART LONG-HAUL DESTINATION
07
0 74470 72699 9
© Francesco Scavullo

Short and blonde—on the cover of *Harper's & Queen*

and for a number of reasons a business climate evolved where fashion clients no longer had to pay the big fees top models earned in the '90s. Models were also replaced on covers by leading actresses and pop culture celebrities.

The online era progressed exponentially. Social media arrived on the scene, and in the past decade went viral. This created a shift in reverse with regard to the earnings of supermodels who began to earn those megabucks once more and appear on covers again as well.

This reversal came about largely because of the kind of communication social media has made possible.

We spend most of our time nowadays in front of computers or looking down at smartphones contacting one another and sharing information like crazy, indicating what we "like" on Facebook, Twitter, Instagram, Pinterest, etc. The great measure of popularity is how many followers you can accumulate. Extreme celebrity and popularity can garner millions of followers.

And how do people generate lots of followers? By constructing an emotional experience for their target audience around a unique identity. The target audience are people who are likely to be interested in you. Your identity can be based on anything: beauty, talent, achievement, or a look, or scandalous behavior, or association with a popular reality show, etc.; along with everything else about you that is associated with your uniqueness like where you're from, the way you dress, what you eat, how you spend your leisure time, people you hang out with, your interests and concerns.

To return to the quote I opened with, branding is about riding the coattails of fame, and it doesn't matter how or why someone becomes famous. All that counts is that instantaneous recognition—awareness is key—and the size of the following it generates on social media.

This phenomenon gave individuals, particularly in the world of entertainment, the opportunity to create their own brands. The ones who are most successful at doing this attract many millions of followers who hang on their every Tweet and Instagram post and can be counted on to follow them to whatever interests and products they become associated with or endorse. Where models are concerned, they can become highly bankable commodities who attract million-dollar cosmetic or designer contracts.

Page 156: Joan Vass campaign

Page 157: My first *Cosmo* cover

Page 158: The grunge cover—*Mademoiselle*

Page 159: Another *Mademoiselle* cover

Page 160: *W* cover with Nadege du Bospertus

Page 161: French *Vogue* in Mexico

Page 162: My American Stroke Association PSA

Page 163: "Together to end stroke" PSA I did for American Heart Association/ American Stroke Association

joan vass usa®

COSMOPOLITAN

THE INTERNATIONAL LANGUAGE OF YOUNG WOMEN

£2 November 1995

Happy,
Healthy,
Exciting
Sex
The **6** steps
to sexual nirvana

**WHEN
NO ONE
LIKES HIM
BUT YOU**

A woman confesses:
"My night in
a male hooker"

BABY-SNATCHING
**HUNDREDS OF
BRITISH WOMEN
ARE THINKING
ABOUT IT
RIGHT NOW**

Cosmo
welcomes
new covergirl
Claudia
Mason

NAKED HOLLYWOOD
Male movie stars talk about *those* nude scenes

All you want to do is have some fun
So why does dating always have to lead to diamonds?

GUARANTEED:
SUCCESS IN LOVE, WORK & LIFE
HOW REORGANISING YOUR HOME WILL REV UP YOUR FUTURE
(believe it!)

**EXCLUSIVE! THE WORLD'S
WEALTHIEST WOMEN**
(but are they *happy*?)

© Bolling Powell

9 770141 055092

11

FEBRUARY 1993 $2.50

Mademois

Spring Fashion—
tough, sweet & sexy

Navy & White
for Now, Forever

20 Diet Foods
That Aren't

Hollywood's
Top Skin Doc
Tells All!

Mademoiselle

JULY 1994
$2.00

love or lust?

Why Guys Dump Girls
THEIR **TRUE** REASONS

How to Make Sex Better
REALLY, **REALLY** BETTER

When Will He Marry Me?
WE'RE **SO** HAPPY!

COOL LOOKS FOR DAY & NIGHT

10 Diet Rules
Made to Be Broken

Is Your Life Totally Out of Control?

A Great Butt
EXERCISES THAT **DO IT**

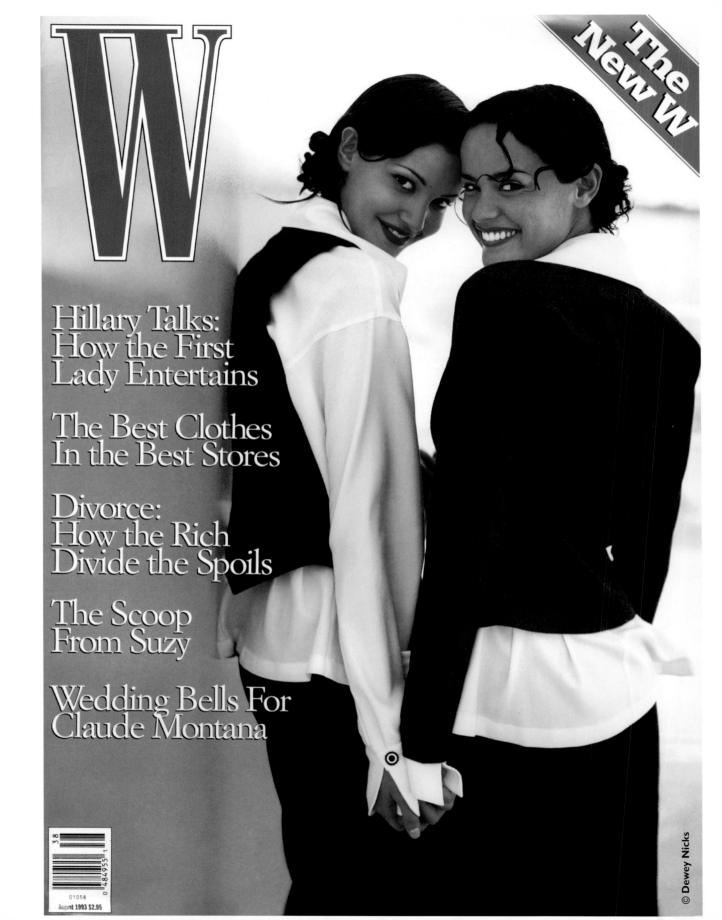

W

The New W

Hillary Talks:
How the First
Lady Entertains

The Best Clothes
In the Best Stores

Divorce:
How the Rich
Divide the Spoils

The Scoop
From Suzy

Wedding Bells For
Claude Montana

August 1993 $2.95

Le buste lacé, ci-contre, dans une combinaison près du corps en coton et viscose, sur une chemise en popeline de coton à large col, créées par Corinne Cobson. Ampleur et motifs, page de droite, pour la chemise en gazar de soie imprimé, signée Gianfranco Ferré, nouée sur un pantalon taille haute en gabardine de coton stretch, signé Plein Sud. Une mine de soleil avec Poudre Bronzante "Indienne" de Caron,

© Javier Vallhonrat

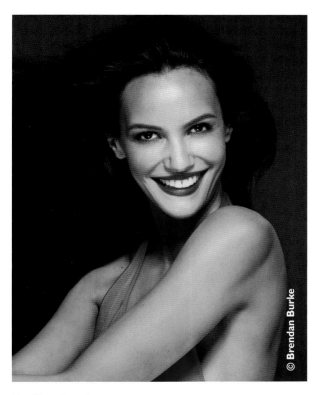

© Brendan Burke

Smiling for the camera

Previous page: **On top of the world in Montmartre, Paris, for** *Vogue*

Good-looking girls with a ton of followers who may not have been competitive as models in an earlier era, are very appealing to model agencies and clients today.

Branding is the super-hot vehicle today for selling *anything*. So it's important for all aspiring models to be aware of its power. Be very aware what is unique about *you* as you go along and grow along. Build on your image, generate a huge following on social media, and voilà, megabuck contracts could follow.

You build on your brand by having things to say and show on social media that relate to your image in some way. You share information, opinions, photos, and videos of yourself and/or others at gatherings and special occasions; comment on relevant events, give advice, welcome follower participation.

Branding has changed the way a model's career can quickly climb. High numbers of followers make a model desirable to clients looking to sell perfumes, clothing, and cosmetics. While models were once considered only muses to fashion clients, social media's influence on a model's public presence has changed the fashion clients' perception of a model to a marketing partner as well as a muse. Simply put, social media has enabled a model to quickly build her brand and therefore given her a new kind of power which has influenced the role she plays in the fashion industry. Branding has brought models' fees back to what they had been in the lucrative 90s.

So raising a models' social media numbers is at the forefront of many model agents' minds today.

Get to know who you are and what is unique about you. Then put it all out there on social media. Generate those numbers of followers, because they can translate into numbers of dollars.

IN CLOSING

You are now armed with invaluable information derived from my career as a supermodel. I've outlined the qualities you need to cultivate, and how to do it, and provided you with the practical information also required to find the supermodel in you. Now, just get out there and do your best. And enjoy the ride!

CLAUDIA'S SCOREBOARD

Gauge your progress with this handy tool!

1 point per item. 100 items total.

A+ - 95 points or better/supermodel status
A - 90 points or better
B - 80 points or better
C - 70 points or better

1. Enjoy performing in front of a camera, practice with friends.

2. Consult fashion media to determine whether you have an interest in the industry.

3. Discuss with parent/guardian the desire to model.

4. If you're not discovered by a scout or in a legit contest, contact the top modeling agencies and ask them for a legitimate affiliate in a city near you if you can't get to one of the major fashion cities right away. Refer to my agency list.

5. Contact the agencies you have chosen, whether in a major fashion city or elsewhere, to find out when they see new talent.

6. Arrange to travel to nearest city where agencies are located. Try to see three to five agencies on one trip.

7. Make travel and lodging arrangements.

8. In the weeks leading up to your visit to modeling agencies, take optimum care of your appearance.

9. Go to the agencies dressed as you normally do, wear minimal makeup, if any, and take your parent with you.

10. Do not sign any agency contract without legal advice.

11. Once signed with a legitimate agency, celebrate!

12 Establish good relationships with your bookers, also called agents and managers. They get you the work.

13 Be responsible. Show up to your castings and bookings on time and ready to work.

14 Book your first modeling job!

15 Receive your first paycheck for modeling!

16 At your age, you'll need chaperones. Learn to appreciate them. They're there for your own good, and soon enough, you won't need them.

17 Let your bookers guide your career and learn from their expertise.

18 If moving around and being expressive in front of the camera doesn't come easy to you, be creative about it, and take a dance or acting class.

19 Catalog and editorial require different styles of modeling. The more work you do, the more you'll get the hang of it. Most importantly, take direction from clients and photographers.

20 Learn from the photographers you work with.

21 Learn from the fashion editors and stylists. They don't just prepare you for the current job, they often book you for future jobs as well.

22 Learn from the designers you work with.

23 Be mindful of client perspectives. ☐

24 Learn from hair and makeup artists how to look your best when you have to do hair and makeup yourself for industry events. ☐

25 Learn from more experienced models you work with. ☐

26 Embrace the fashion industry in its entirety, as it teaches you how to be a professional working model. ☐

27 Be sure to keep up with school assignments. ☐

28 Maintain balance in your life. Keep up with friends and peer group activities as you need to. ☐

29 Have your own bank account separate from your parents. ☐

30 It is important for you to appear on some covers. Discuss with head booker. ☐

31 You get your first cover! ☐

32 If you're not already on social media, get on it. Build your brand. ☐

33 Learn from more experienced models about respecting your limits and when to say "No" to demands that feel inappropriate to you. ☐

34 Be aware of The Model Alliance, a not-for-profit labor group for models working in the American fashion industry. ☐

35 Keep abreast of the continuing attempt to establish a labor union to protect models' welfare and rights.

36 Eat healthy foods to help sustain your looks.

37 Always keep your skin well moisturized. Use SPF.

38 You'll be going to Europe for shoots. Get to know your European bookers.

39 Familiarize yourself with how to get around the fashion capitals.

40 . . . the New York City subway system.

41 . . . the Paris Metro.

42 . . . the London Underground.

43 . . . in Milan, it's mostly taxis (until you're a supermodel being driven around by drivers in all cities).

44 Generate lists of recommended dentists, doctors, and other professionals in fashion capitals where you may spend extended periods of time.

45 Your first residence away from home will likely be a shared models' apartment maintained by your agency and paid for out of your earnings.

46 Get some fashion shows under your belt, and begin to develop career-long relationships with important fashion designers.

47 Complete high school and graduate. ☐

48 Establish good working relationships with the photographers, particularly the important ones. They are instrumental in building your career from model to supermodel. ☐

49 Do lots of editorial jobs. They lead to the big money jobs. ☐

50 Ah, you've gotten your first big money job! Celebrate! ☐

51 Develop healthy habits to look and feel your best. ☐

52 Keep in shape, with any form of exercise that appeals to you. ☐

53 Keep in shape with healthy eating habits. Eat lots of veggies and whole grains and take it easy on the sugar. ☐

54 Drink lots of water. ☐

55 Enjoy your life! That will help you be your most vibrant in front of the camera. ☐

56 You get your second cover. ☐

57 Continue the good relationship you've developed with your head booker. ☐

58 . . . in New York. ☐

59 . . . in Paris. ☐

60 . . . in London.

61 . . . in Milan.

62 . . . and in any of the other fashion cities.

63 Maintain good relationships with all the clients.

64 Land your first runway season in Paris.

65 . . . in Milan.

66 . . . in New York.

67 . . . in London.

68 Develop good working relationships with the fashion designers, photographers, and stylists so they will keep booking you for future jobs, which is how you become a supermodel.

69 If you feel you should have a shot at an opportunity that has eluded you, don't take "No" for an answer. If one tactic fails, try another. Be creative.

70 Keep a healthy perspective about yourself and your job. Keep yourself grounded in order to make the most of your career, and to see it last for as long as it can.

71 Continue to pursue covers. They will position you for lucrative contracts.

72 You get your third cover.

73 Continue to pursue advertising campaigns. They will also help position you for lucrative contracts.

74 You land your first lucrative contract, e.g., you're signed to be the face of a major cosmetic brand!

75 Modeling for commercials and fashion films isn't that different from modeling for still photo shoots. In both cases, the product you are selling will determine your performance.

76 Learn how to protect and invest your money from a trusted money manager. You need your money to help sustain your image in the industry as well as for your future.

77 As your career gains momentum, continue taking editorial jobs as well as the higher-paying jobs. Along with covers and advertising jobs, editorial jobs will help keep you artistically relevant in the industry and will therefore keep you in the running for the more lucrative work like the cosmetic and perfume contracts.

78 Get your driver's license. Knowing how to drive is an important stepping-stone into adulthood.

79 When you can afford to do so, get your own residence.

80 Continue to keep in shape with exercise and healthy eating habits.

81   Try not to use drugs and alcohol to the extent that it ruins your looks.

82   Practice safe sex.

83   Sexual promiscuity within the industry is tricky. Be careful who you sleep with to guard your professional reputation.

84   Attend fashion events to maintain your professional status.

85   Also attend high-profile non-industry events.

86   Thank-you cards and gifts are good business. Keep sending them.

87   Christmas cards and gifts to your significant clients and to your bookers are de rigueur.

88   As college years approach, decide whether you want a college education.

89   Decide whether or not to defer a college education to when your high-earning modeling years are over.

90   Be aware of possible career interests after modeling.

91   Keep in touch with the contacts you make within the industry, as they may be helpful in facilitating your next career.

92 Also keep in touch with non-industry contacts for the same reason.

93 This may be your one opportunity to make a lot of money. Spend and enjoy, but save as well.

94 Have fun! Modeling is a once-in-a-lifetime opportunity that won't last forever. Enjoy all the perks the business has to offer.

95 If it's recommended in the industry that you get plastic surgery of any kind, be sure you select a reputable surgeon who specializes in what you need.

96 The same rule applies to orthodontics.

97 Think creatively about promoting yourself.

98 When you have gained some momentum in your career, hire a publicist to help you keep your name and face out there to build your image and position you to command top dollar.

99 Be sure that your agency is doing their very best for you. If they're not, consider switching agencies.

100 Think positively. Learn to see the glass as half full rather than as half empty. This attitude facilitates success.

APPENDIX OF TERMS AND NAMES

Alateen	Part of Al-Anon Family Groups, it's a fellowship of young Al-Anon members, usually teenagers, whose lives have been affected by someone else's drinking or by any other issues. It provides powerful support.
atelier	A workshop or studio, especially one used by an artist or designer.
au courant	French for "current."
Boston Brace	A back brace used primarily for the treatment of idiopathic scoliosis in children and adolescents.
Bloomingdale's	An American upscale chain of department stores.
brasserie	An informal restaurant, especially one in France or modeled on a French one and with a large selection of drinks.
Baudelaire	Was a French poet, essayist, and art critic.
chausson aux pommes	A French pastry similar to an apple turnover.

Fiera	The Fiera Milano, an exhibition center in Milan that hosts fashion events.
George Balanchine	Was one of the 20th century's foremost choreographers of ballet, cofounded both the New York City Ballet company and The School of American Ballet.
Gyrotonics	The Gyrotonic method is an original and unique movement practice which has roots in Yoga, Tai Chi, and dance. These carefully crafted sequences create balance, efficiency, strength, and flexibility.
GED	The General Educational Development test, designed for people who did not graduate from high school but want a certificate equivalent to the traditional high school diploma.
haute couture	French for "high fashion," haute couture refers to the creation of exclusive custom-fitted clothing.
La La Land	Los Angeles.
l'attitude des Parisiens	The attitude of Parisians.
Les Fleurs du Mal	A volume of French poetry by Charles Baudelaire. First published in 1857, it was important in the symbolist and modernist movements. The poems deal with themes relating to decadence and eroticism.
Lincoln Center	Lincoln Center for the Performing Arts is a 16.3-acre complex of buildings in the Lincoln Square neighborhood of Manhattan in New York City.
Mlle	Abbreviation for "Mademoiselle" which is French for "Miss."
Musée Rodin	The Musée Rodin, French for "Rodin Museum" in Paris, France, is a museum that was opened in 1919, dedicated to the works of the French sculptor Auguste Rodin.
patisserie	A type of French or Belgian bakery that specializes in pastries and sweets.

Philippe Petit A French high-wire artist who gained fame in 1974 for his high-wire walk between the Twin Towers of the World Trade Center in New York City, on the morning of August 7.

Pilates A system of mind-body exercise using a floor mat or a variety of equipment. It teaches body awareness, good posture, and easy, graceful movement. It also improves flexibility, agility, and economy of motion.

pommes frites French for "French fries."

prêt-à-porter French for ready-to-wear, factory-made clothing, sold in finished condition, in standardized sizes.

"Roofies" A benzodiazepine drug that is illegal in the United States but is used elsewhere as a hypnotic and in anesthesia. It is popularly known as the "date rape drug" because its ability to cause semi-consciousness and memory blackouts has led to its association with unwanted sexual encounters.

silver screen The movies.

tabac In French-speaking regions, a shop licensed to sell tobacco products. It also sells newspapers, telephone cards, and postage stamps. A café can be a tabac but a tabac isn't necessarily a café.

The Cloisters The Cloisters is a museum located in Fort Tryon Park in the Washington Heights section of Upper Manhattan, New York City. It is a branch of the Metropolitan Museum of Art.

1er arrondissement The 1st arrondissement. Paris, France, is divided into twenty arrondissements.

APPENDIX OF THE TOP 13 NEW YORK MODELING AGENCIES (LISTED ALPHABETICALLY)

- DNA Models
- Elite New York City
- Ford Models
- IMG
- New York Model Management
- Next New York
- One Management
- Supreme Management
- The Lions
- The Society Management
- Trump Management
- Wilhelmina New York
- Women Management

PHOTOGRAPHY CREDITS

Front Cover: Photographer: Renée Cox. An early modeling test, 1986.

Back Cover: Photographer: Christophe Kutner. British *Elle*, 1995.

Author Photo: Photographer: Olivia Owen, 2015.

Chapter Title Photos: Photographer: Olivia Owen, 2015. Model: Phillippa Steele. Makeup artist: Colleen O'Neill, 2015.

Page 2: Photographer: Unknown. First modeling test, 1987.

Page 4: Photographer: Robert Erdmann. *Miss Vogue* cover, 1987.

Page 7: Photographer: Unknown. Paris *Match*.

Page 8: Photographer: Jim Varriale. An American *Vogue* promotion.

Page 11: Photographer: Mario Testino. Italian *Vogue*.

Page 12: Photographer: Bruce Weber. *Lei* magazine.

Page 14: Photographer: Mario Testino. British *Elle*.

Page 16: Photographer: Mario Testino. Italian *Vogue*.

Page 17: Photographer: Martin Brading. Sportmax campaign.

Page 20: Photographer: Andrew Macpherson. British *Elle* cover, 1992.

Page 22: Photographer: Christophe Kutner. French *Elle* cover, 1995.

Page 24: Photographer: Gilles Bensimon. French *Elle* cover, 1993.

Page 25: Photographer: Tyen. German *Elle* cover, 1991.

Page 29: Photographer: Max Vadukul. *Vogue* Paris cover, 1992.

Page 30: Photographer: Tyen. A Versace promotion.

Page 32: Photographer: Tyen. British *Vogue*, 1991.

Page 35: Photographer: Matthew Rolston. *Vogue España* cover, 1995.

Page 38: Photographers: Avedon, Jay Zuckerkorn, Toscani, Jim Varriale. Elite model card.

Page 48: Photographer: Patrick Demarchelier. Istante campaign.

Page 50: Photographer: Peter Lindbergh. British *Vogue* cover, 1992.

Page 51: Photographer: David Bailey. British *Vogue* cover, 1992.

Page 52: Photographer: Guzman. Louis Vuitton campaign, 1996.

Page 55: Photographer: Guzman. Louis Vuitton campaign, 1996.

Page 57: Photographer: Guzman. Louis Vuitton campaign, 1996.

Page 58: Photographer: Wayne Maser. Club Monaco campaign.

Page 60: Photographer: Tyen. Ferre Jeans campaign.

Page 61: Photographer: Pamela Hanson. German *Vogue*.

Page 63: Photographer: Bruce Weber. American *Vogue*, 1992.

Page 65: Photographer: Patrick Demarchelier. Harper's *Bazaar*, 1992.

Page 67: Photographer: Patrick Demarchelier. Harper's *Bazaar*, 1992.

Page 69: Photographer: Unknown. Versace fashion show.

Page 70: Photographers: Unknown.

Page 72: Photographers: Unknown. American *Vogue* beauty clips.

Page 74: Photographers: Unknown.

Page 74: Photographers: Roxanne Lowit, Guy Marineau. American *Vogue*.

Pages 86–87: Photographer: Hannah Khymych, 2011.

Page 88: Photographer: Christophe Kutner. British *Elle*, 1995.

Page 89: Photographer: Christophe Kutner. British *Elle*, 1995.

Page 91: Photographer: Christophe Kutner. British *Elle*, 1995.

Page 92: Photographer: Thierry Le Goues. French *Glamour*.

Page 93: Photographer: Walter Chin. French *Vogue*, 1996.

Page 94: Photographer: Bruce Weber. American *Vogue*, 1992.

Page 95: Photographer: Pamela Hanson. British *Vogue*.

Page 97: Photographer: Thierry Le Goues. French *Glamour*.

Page 99: Photographer: Andre Rau. Spanish *Vogue*.

Page 104: Photographer: Marc Hispard. French *Elle*.

Page 107,108: Photographer: Javier Vallhonrat. French *Vogue*.

Page 111: Photographer: Robert Erdmann. *Mademoiselle*.

Page 112: Photographer: Regan Cameron. Italian *Marie Claire*.

Pages 114, 117: Photographer: Satoshi Saikusa. Italian *Marie Claire*.

Page 118: Photographer: Tyen. *Madame Figaro* cover.

Page 122: Photographer: Angelo Pennetta. *Love* magazine, 2010.

Page 124: Photographer: Willy Vanderperre. Russian *Vogue*, 2010.

Page 125: Photographer: Tiziano Magni. British *Elle*, 1991.

Page 127: Photographer: Enrique Badulescu. British *Elle*, 1992.

Page 128: Photographer: Christophe Kutner. British *Elle*, 1995.

Page 131: Photographer: Sante D'Orazio. British *Vogue*, 1993.

Pages 132–133: Photographer: Sante D'Orazio. British *Vogue*, 1993.

Page 134: Photographer: Enrique Badulescu. British *Elle*, 1992.

Page 138: Photographer: Max Vadukul. American *Vogue*.

Pages 140–141: Photographer: Bruce Weber. American *Vogue*, 1992.

Page 143: Photographer: Enrique Badulescu. British *Elle*, 1992.

Page 146: Photographer: Walter Chin. *Mademoiselle*, 1993.

Page 147: Photographer: Pamela Hanson. German *Vogue*.

Page 152: Photographer: Karl Lagerfeld. Fendi campaign.

Page 153: Photographer: Tyen. Christian Lacroix campaign.

Page 154: Photographer: Francesco Scavullo. *Harper's & Queen* cover, 1994.

Page 156: Photographer: Javier Vallhonrat. Joan Vass campaign.

Page 157: Photographer: Bolling Powell. British *Cosmopolitan* cover, 1995.

Page 158: Photographer: Walter Chin. *Mademoiselle* cover, 1993.

Page 159: Photographer: Walter Chin. *Mademoiselle* cover, 1994.

Page 160: Photographer: Dewey Nicks. *W* cover.

Page 161: Photographer: Javier Vallhonrat. French *Vogue*.

Pages 162, 163: Photographer: Olivia Owen. American Stroke Association's PSA, 2015.

Page 164: Photographer: Pamela Hanson. German *Vogue*.

Page 165: Photographer: Brendan Burke, 2012.

Page 168: Photographer: Pamela Hanson. German *Vogue*.

ABOUT THE AUTHOR

© Olivia Owen

Claudia Mason is a supermodel, actor, producer of theater and film, and a writer. Born and raised in New York City, Mason began studying ballet at the age of five and trained at the prestigious School of American Ballet. It was during her time as a dance student at New York City's Fiorello H. LaGuardia High School of Music & Art and Performing Arts that she was discovered by a scout from the Elite Modeling Agency.

Mason went on to become one of the world's top models working with designers including Yves Saint Laurent, Karl Lagerfeld, Versace, Armani, Gucci, Valentino, Marc Jacobs, and Calvin Klein. She was featured on the covers of such magazines as *Vogue, W, Mademoiselle, Elle, Cosmopolitan,* and numerous foreign publications. She starred in many prestigious fashion campaigns for Versace, Anne Klein, and Fendi, among others. She has worked with all the top photographers including Richard Avedon, Bruce Weber, and Mario Testino.

Mason has appeared in film, TV, and theater, producing and starring in a highly acclaimed LADCC-nominated production of Tennessee Williams's *Orpheus Descending.* She currently has a TV series in development with Frogwater Media. Recently she was named a spokesperson for the American Stroke Association. She herself is a stroke survivor, having suffered a minor stoke from a freak accident. Mason has fully recovered but remains devoted to spreading the word about stroke prevention, early signs, and treatment. She lives in New York City.